Knowing Obadiah

a Christian Women's Bible Commentary

Series:

A Fire and a Flame

APRIL W GARDNER

God bless +
thank you!

Big Spring Press

And the light of Israel shall be for a fire,
and his Holy One for a flame.
Isaiah 10:17a

And the house of Jacob shall be a fire,
and the house of Joseph a flame,
and the house of Esau for stubble.
Obadiah 18

Praise for *Knowing Obadiah*

April dives deep in *Knowing Obadiah*, exploring the nooks and crannies of this incredibly short book of the Bible. Not only does she bring out a greater understanding of the book of Obadiah, but she also explores the start of it all. April's work has given me a new perspective on these events and the history of Edom as a whole, a perspective that I am sure I will keep coming back too.

–Rebekah Gyger,
archaeologist and author of the Biblical novel, *Rahab: Hidden Scars*

April learned Bible study skills from her father's pulpit and at her mother's knee. Later, she learned the many nuances of human relationships as she penned books of Christian fiction. In this study of the little book of Obadiah, she has combined her skills to present us with a many-faceted view of the prophetic and historic account of God's dealing with Edom as well as an inciteful view of the family dynamics which led to God's dealing with both Edom and Israel. I know you will enjoy this study as much as I have.

–Charlotte Lowe,
International Board of Jewish Missions

KNOWING
OBADIAH

And the Kingdom Shall Be the Lord's
A Christian Women's Bible Commentary

APRIL W GARDNER

Big Spring Press

Series Details

A Fire and a Flame

- *A Hope Fulfilled*, a novella of biblical Edom and
  Obadiah's prophecy

- *Knowing Obadiah*, a Christian Women's Bible
  Commentary

- *But in Mount Zion*, a companion study for
  Knowing Obadiah (personal or small group)

Can be read in any order.
Learn more and purchase at
www.aprilgardner.com/fireandflame.

Series Dedication

To the women of my small group at
Oakwood Baptist.
As I wrote, each of you was on my mind.
Thank you for your unfailing love and support
and for your countless prayers.

Knowing Obadiah: A Christian Women's Bible Commentary
©2023 by April W Gardner

Cover design: Indie Cover Design

Library of Congress Control Number: 2023913785
ISBN-13: 978-1-945831-39-3

Published by Big Spring Press
San Antonio, Texas
Printed in the United States of America.

Contents

Introduction

In late December 2021, while deciding on a Bible reading goal for the upcoming year, I pondered which sections of the Bible I knew least. The minor prophets came to mind right off, then camped there as I asked myself what I knew about these little books.

I'd heard a million sermons preached from one or another of them over the years, but could I give even a one-sentence summary on any of the twelve? That question required a moment's thought, which produced Jonah and the big fish, Hosea and his harlot wife, Joel and the locusts, Amos and… Uh, er, uh…

This was a problem. After burning some brain cells on the matter, I finally hung my head and admitted I was a minor failure. If I'd been tested right then on the minor prophets, I would have received a big red F.

How was this possible? I'm a missionary's kid who never missed a church service, for goodness' sake. This was unacceptable. I had an MK reputation to uphold.

Kidding, kidding. But the point remains. After 4.5 decades in church, I should be able to state every book's title and theme. At a minimum. Anything less is spiritual laziness.

With that challenge in mind, I hitched up my trousers and set to work. My task? One minor prophet a month. I would read each one again and again, really drilling them home, absorbing their messages and banishing my spiritual "shame."

By April, and my fourth read of Obadiah, I stared at my Bible, the verses swimming before me, and admitted to a second problem—despite my faithful rereading, the first four books were all running together in a mental smear of prophety messages. Warning, judgment, doom, gloom. There was hope in there, too, of course. Praise God. And a harlot wife. I had that one down. But I was no closer to being able to distinguish them, to really *understand* the books with any kind of true ownership.

Since I'm a goal-girl, it made me a little sad to set aside my twelve-prophet year, but there was no getting around it. If this was going to work, I would have to go deeper, get messier, put on my work gloves and knee pads and start digging.

New goal! Understand Obadiah. I'd worry about the rest once I had this one down. Fifteen months and two written books later, here we are.

When I cracked open the first Obadiah commentary from my church library, writing on the topic wasn't on my radar, but once the book's history and truths began sinking in, my writer's instincts naturally fired up. Soon, I was so excited about what I was learning (and marveling over how I'd missed it after so many invested church hours), I decided I had to share. There *had* to be others out there like me who'd overlooked this amazing little gem of a book.

But who am I to do any writing on the subject? No one, really. As mentioned, I grew up in church and on the mission field. There was a little Bible college in there before I got my Mrs. degree and joined my new USAF husband overseas. I've led women's groups at church, worked as a children's ministry leader, written Christian fiction, and over the years, filled about every volunteer position a church can have. But really, I'm just the next girl on the church pew. Nothing special.

I have no formal theological education. Only a curious mind, a love of learning, and a long-standing devotion to Christ. Because of that, I've approached this study from the seat beside yours at home, as if we had our Bibles open on our laps, coffee mugs in hand, and were chatting about the things we're discovering while we read.

We're in this together, my friend, learning as we go, understanding we won't have all the answers and some of the ones we arrive at could very well have other acceptable answers. We'll leave the uncertainties in God's hands and cling to the facts—He is sovereign, His plan for eternity is perfect, and He wants us to trust Him with it.

While we're on the subject, as far as studies go, Obadiah might be one of the stickiest prophecies to write about definitively because we can't know for sure when it was written or, consequently, which events it's describing. The point of the study, though, isn't to walk away saying, "I have all the answers" (Only God has those, right?). The point is to be able to say, "I know the book inside-out, its message and all its possible interpretations." I'm confident you'll be able to do that by the end.

You'll also understand how and why Edom is the object of God's wrath. You'll see how the book, like every other prophecy, contains a message of warning, judgment, and hope, and how (unlike the rest of the prophets) the first two (warning and judgment) are for a pagan nation while the last (hope) is for Judah.

If you've thumbed through this book and wondered how in the world so much can be written about twenty-one verses, trust me, it's entirely possible. This most minor of minor prophets is absolutely *packed* with treasure waiting to be unburied and hugged with all the enthusiasm of our gold-loving friend Scrooge McDuck. Toss in its background and its implications for the future, and you've got yourself a chunky commentary and study.

Speaking of study, *Knowing Obadiah* is not topical, meaning it doesn't cover any set topic related to spiritual growth (but it does cover topics as they arrive in context). Instead, I take an exegesis approach, which digs for original meaning, versus applying modern interpretation.

This commentary will force you out of your comfy chair and into Obadiah's history and culture. As best we can, we'll be taking on the author's perspective of the world, looking at the text's setting and purpose (and so much more!) through his lens.

We'll be going deep, but if you'd like to go deeper yet, consider the other two books in the A Fire and a Flame series. If you want support material that expands on themes in this book, you might be interested in the companion study and interactive workbook, *But in Mount Zion*. It works for both personal and small-group settings. With it, you'll discover how the message of Obadiah speaks to your life in a personal way.

And for those of you who enjoy biblical fiction, this series includes a novella based on the (assumed) historical events surrounding Obadiah. In *A Hope Fulfilled*, God uses a Hebrew slave woman named Tikvah to bring about Edom's destruction. Highly fictionalized, it imagines how events might have unfolded during the fulfillment of Obadiah's prophecy. It brings the book's setting to life and promises to deepen your understanding of Edom's message of doom.

Regardless of how many books in the A Fire and a Flame series you read, I pray that through your study of Obadiah, the Spirit speaks to you in a powerful way. I pray the truths found in it will burrow permanently into your heart and mind, so that if ever you're asked, "What's Obadiah about?" you'll have a ready and confident answer, one that resonates in your soul.

Because He lives,
April

OBADIAH

Judgment Comes for Edom

1 The vision of Obadiah.
Thus saith the Lord God concerning Edom;
We have heard a rumour from the Lord,
and an ambassador is sent among the heathen,
Arise ye, and let us rise up against her in battle.
2 Behold, I have made thee small among the heathen:
thou art greatly despised.
3 The pride of thine heart hath deceived thee,
thou that dwellest in the clefts of the rock,
whose habitation is high; that saith in his heart,
Who shall bring me down to the ground?
4 Though thou exalt thyself as the eagle,
and though thou set thy nest among the stars,
thence will I bring thee down, saith the Lord.
5 If thieves came to thee,
if robbers by night, (how art thou cut off!)
would they not have stolen till they had enough?
if the grape gatherers came to thee,
would they not leave some grapes?
6 How are the things of Esau searched out!
how are his hidden things sought up!
7 All the men of thy confederacy
have brought thee even to the border:
the men that were at peace with thee have deceived thee,
and prevailed against thee;
they that eat thy bread have laid a wound under thee:
there is none understanding in him.

8 Shall I not in that day, saith the Lord,
even destroy the wise men out of Edom,
and understanding out of the mount of Esau?
9 And thy mighty men, O Teman, shall be dismayed,
to the end that every one of the mount of Esau
may be cut off by slaughter.

Edom's Offense against Judah
10 For thy violence against thy brother Jacob
shame shall cover thee, and thou shalt be cut off for ever.
11 In the day that thou stoodest on the other side,
in the day that the strangers carried away captive his forces,
and foreigners entered into his gates,
and cast lots upon Jerusalem, even thou wast as one of them.
12 But thou shouldest not have looked on the day of thy
brother in the day that he became a stranger;
neither shouldest thou have rejoiced over the children of
Judah in the day of their destruction; neither shouldest thou
have spoken proudly in the day of distress.
13 Thou shouldest not have entered into the gate
of my people in the day of their calamity;
yea, thou shouldest not have looked
on their affliction in the day of their calamity, nor have laid
hands on their substance in the day of their calamity;
14 Neither shouldest thou have stood in the crossway
to cut off those of his that did escape;
neither shouldest thou have delivered up
those of his that did remain in the day of distress.
15 For the day of the Lord is near upon all the heathen:
as thou hast done, it shall be done unto thee:
thy reward shall return upon thine own head.
16 For as ye have drunk upon my holy mountain,
so shall all the heathen drink continually,
yea, they shall drink, and they shall swallow down,
and they shall be as though they had not been.

The Day of the Lord
17 But upon mount Zion shall be deliverance,
and there shall be holiness;
and the house of Jacob shall possess their possessions.

17

18 And the house of Jacob shall be a fire,
and the house of Joseph a flame,
and the house of Esau for stubble,
and they shall kindle in them, and devour them;
and there shall not be any remaining of the house of Esau;
for the Lord hath spoken it.
19 And they of the south shall possess the mount of Esau;
and they of the plain the Philistines:
and they shall possess the fields of Ephraim,
and the fields of Samaria: and Benjamin shall possess Gilead.
20 And the captivity of this host of the children of Israel
shall possess that of the Canaanites, even unto Zarephath;
and the captivity of Jerusalem, which is in Sepharad,
shall possess the cities of the south.
21 And saviours shall come up on mount Zion
to judge the mount of Esau;
and the kingdom shall be the Lord's

Part 1

MEET
the
PLAYERS

1

Bird's Eye Verses

And your eyes shall see, and you shall say,
The Lord will be magnified from the border of Israel.
Malachi 1:5

Last week in my Wednesday night Awana class, I tasked my five fifth graders with collectively writing out as many books of the Bible as they could remember. They hopped to it, heads bent together as they worked.

"Genesis, Exodus, Leviticus," said Lisa, the scribe of the group.

"Don't forget Matthew!" Matthew contributed.

"Salms," "Efeseans," and "the Solomon guy" went down on the paper along with "all the Johns."

I beamed at their eagerness, Awana bucks at the ready to reward their efforts. When the flow ebbed to a trickle, I helped them along by pointing out that they hadn't remembered the book that starts with the letter O. They looked at each other, brows scrunched, then at me.

Joshua, ever the intrepid one, voiced the question written on every face at the table. "There's one with an O?"

A few months ago, before I began my study of the minor prophets, I probably would have made the same face. Little wonder, since Obadiah consists of a grand total of twenty-one verses. It's the shortest book in the Old Testament and the second shortest in the Bible. Even so, it packs a huge message, one I'm sad to have missed for so many years.

"Yep," I replied to the kids. "It's one of the minor prophets."

That clue didn't jiggle loose any memories, even though they gave it their best head-scratching effort. When I finally gave them the name, they all made sounds of "Oooh." The book's name was familiar, but they couldn't bring it to mind or say what it was about. The poor book, Obadiah, just doesn't get the recognition its prophecy deserves—at least not from modern Christians.

At the time of its writing, however, I imagine the prophet's message made a huge splash. After all, what better news for the destroyed kingdom of Judah than to hear that the contributors to their downfall would be punished beyond oppression, beyond destruction? No, nothing as simple as devastation for the Edomites.

In payment for their actions against Judah, Edom would become "greatly despised" (Obad. 2), covered in shame, and "cut off forever" (10). Their own deeds would return on their heads (15), and, unlike Judah and Israel, to whom God always left a remnant, there would be no survivor left standing (18). Don't mess with God's Chosen People, y'all. Seriously, God is *not* cool with that.

Supporting Israel can be an important lesson to glean from this little book, but there's so much more to be had. One of my goals for this study is to further your grasp on how history and the major players in Israel's lineage knit together.

God really is the master weaver. So impressive. The book's backstory, including the bad blood between the Edomites and Israelites, goes back a thousand years, all the way to Isaac and Rebekah's twins, Jacob and Esau.

Because of that, the first half of this study will be dedicated to understanding the book's context in history and discovering God's marvelous hand in it all the way through. I trust you'll find the story and promises related in these twenty-one verses as fascinating and encouraging as I do and more familiar than expected.

Since I'm a girl who likes to know what's coming, outlines and bullet points are my jam. No surprises for me, please and thank you. So, over the next five chapters, here's what we'll be covering.

1. Meet the players (v. 1)
    a. Key verses
    b. Who's Obadiah
    c. When's Obadiah

      d. Obadiah's audience

      e. Introducing Edom

2. Book's origin story (10a)

      a. Jacob and Esau, the twins who started it all

      b. Thefts, blessings, and threats

      c. Esau's "blessing" fulfilled in Edom

3. Edom's violence against Judah

      a. Judah's downfall (10a)

      b. Edom's hand in it (11–14)

      c. Ezekiel and Jeremiah weigh in

4. Edom's violence repaid

      a. Arrogance and foolish boasting (2–4)

      b. Wrath prophesied (5–7)

      c. Wrath played out (8–9, 10b, 15–16)

5. Judah's ultimate victory

      a. Three blessings (17–18)

      b. Three promises (17–18)

      c. Jesus Messiah will reign (19–21)

After glancing at the outline, you probably picked up on two repeated E words: Esau and Edom.

Esau, Jacob's hairy twin.

Edom, the nation that formed from his descendants.

Not your typical Bible study topics, huh? That's okay. Different is good. It means we're going deeper, digging past the comfortably familiar passages and books.

If you're looking for a tried-and-true Sunday school story, the Genesis account of Jacob and Esau is probably at the top of the list. From there, most of us take the right-hand fork in the road and follow Jacob's descendants into the formation of Israel and, later, Judah.

We forget all about Esau, his sons, and his sons' sons, called Edomites. We even forget to connect Edom with the twins of Father Abraham days. And have you ever tied the Edomites with those who threatened Jesus, Peter, and Paul? I'm going to assume not. That ends here, my friend. We're taking the left fork, which leads down Esau's path.

In fact, over the next chapters, we'll get so far down into the weeds of Esau/Edom and Jacob/Judah's thousand-year interactions, the sky might disappear for a bit. But have no fear, you *did* pick up a study on Obadiah, and when that sky reappears, our "eyes shall see, and [we] shall say, The Lord will be magnified from the border of Israel" (Mal. 1:5).

To some of us, Edom is an afterthought. Not so with Israel and certainly not for God. From Genesis to Malachi, from the first book of the Old Testament to the last, the Lord "loved" Israel and "hated" Edom (Mal. 1:2–3).

Here, the words *love* and *hate* don't mean affection and lack of. They mean "choosing for a special purpose[1]" and *not*. Yes, Israel is destined to play a particular role in world history, but God's eternal plan acted out on Earth extends further than the nation of Israel. The plan here is to get a clear depiction of that through Edom and His treatment of their wickedness.

Better yet, through Edom, God emphasizes His loyalty to His children, to those who choose to follow Him and His ways.

That's me! And that's you, sister. Regardless of our earthly heritage, that's *anyone* who places their trust in Jesus as Savior, as the final verses of Obadiah (17–21) so gloriously state.

But I'm getting way ahead of myself. All in good time. For now, settle in for this fresh look at Esau, Edom, and their role in God's perfect plan.

What's up first? Read the book!

Because Obadiah is so short, I recommend you read it through several times. Personally, I listened to it being read aloud from my Bible app every morning while I dressed for the day, often hitting replay to listen to it again and again. I now have the book practically memorized. Bonus.

Confession. When I first read Obadiah, it didn't make much sense or seem to promise much in the way of take-away content. Maybe I'm a special kind of dense, but while I grasped phrases and concepts, I mostly didn't know which way to interpret some of the passages. Especially those last five.

Are the verses talking about Edom or Israel? (All the theys and thems made my head spin.) Is Obadiah referencing past events, present day (his), or is he prophesying about events yet to come (his or ours?)? Questions, questions, questions.

It wasn't until I'd consumed several commentaries that it began to make sense. Then, with a dozen lightbulbs going off over my head, I realized the book's length is no reflection of its complexity.

As I studied the book a verse at a time, my daily readings became clearer and clearer. There were a lot of *ooohh* and *ah ha* moments. By the time I'd finished my research, I had a fuller understanding of ancient biblical history and the relationships between neighboring nations. I had also uncovered another layer of God's awesomeness and had received a stark reminder that *God is sovereign.* In short, I came to love the book.

I pray the same for you. By the end of this study, you'll be an Edom and Obadiah pro, too. I promise. So hang tight, my friend. Trust the process and read on.

Key Verses

Our two key verses for Obadiah cover both God's judgment and His redemption. Declarations of judgment against Edom, as well as the reasons for it, make up the lion's share of the book.

Promises of redemption and restoration for Israel slide in at the end like punctuation. An exclamation mark, if you ask me. "And the kingdom will be the LORD'S," Obadiah finishes in verse 21. Makes a girl want to whoop a victory shout.

So few words. Such a powerful statement. And so simply delivered. "It's mine," says God through Obadiah. He doesn't need speeches to get His point across. He always gets the last word, and

His Word is *fact*. The kingdom will be as He said. His.

God's indisputable rule over time, as well the events involving humankind, is a constantly repeated truth in Scripture. Hundreds of years before Obadiah picked up his quill, King David was singing about it in Psalm 9. This song can safely be considered prophetic, especially when cast in the light of the tragic events described in Obadiah, as well as God's vow of justice.

> The Lord also will be a refuge for the oppressed, a refuge in times of trouble. And they that know thy name will put their trust in thee: for thou, Lord, hast not forsaken them that seek thee. Sing praises to the Lord, which dwelleth in Zion: declare among the people his doings. When he maketh inquisition for blood, he remembereth them: he forgetteth not the cry of the humble. (Ps. 9:9–12)

You can bet the captive Jews of Obadiah's day were singing this psalm to keep the faith. They would have clung to it as they read Obadiah's prophecy and looked forward to the day the injustices against them would be avenged by a supreme God.

This study's key verses touch on those exact topics.

Key Verse 1
Judgment against those who oppose God's children: "For thy violence against thy

27

brother Jacob shame shall cover thee, and thou shalt be cut off for ever" (Obad. 10).

Key Verse 2
Deliverance for His children: "And saviours shall come up on mount Zion to judge the mount of Esau; and the kingdom shall be the Lord's" (Obad. 21).

Obadiah reminds us that life's disasters are not final. Restoration will come to those who seek the Lord, even if that's not until "kingdom come."
Great is thy faithfulness, Lord, unto us.

Pop Quiz:
Read Obadiah then write the number of a verse that:

    1) intrigues you: _____
    2) confuses you: _____
    3) encourages you: _____

2

Meet and Greet

The vision of Obadiah...
Obadiah 1a

Hey there! Come on in. Welcome, welcome. I'm so glad you decided to join us on this journey of discovering Obadiah. I'm positive you'll leave enlightened and encouraged.

Grab a coffee and a donut from the table there and come right this way. Before we begin, there are two important people you should meet.

Person the First

You might have already met this first one. In fact, He might be a longtime friend. Hope so!

If not...

Dear woman, I present Jesus of Nazareth. He lived some 2,000 years ago on Earth, but today, He's the Keeper of my soul. He's also my Savior, my King, and my dearest Friend. Mine. All mine.

And yet, somehow, in His perfect amazingness, He's also an all-mine Savior, King, Keeper, and Friend to a million others. And He wants to be yours, too.

While we're doing introductions, I should probably mention that He's earned the distinguished titles of "world's most perfect man" and "only man to ever defeat death." Those titles (and so many others) were possible because He's both man and God. For the Bible's say on that, see John 3:16, John 14:6, and I John 5:20.

Yep, Jesus is THE God (Col. 2:9).

Despite that, despite His titles and incomparable achievements, He's right here with us, and He wants to be *your* Savior, King, and Friend. Although many churches depict Christ hanging on a cross, the only thing ongoing about His death is the grace and forgiveness that come from it (1 John 1:9), both of which are available to you free of charge. He died once and for all, and He extends grace and forgiveness as if they were priceless gifts.

I'd love to put them into your hands, but only you can accept them. They're the most important gifts you'll ever receive and not just because they offer a fuller, more soul-enriching life on Earth, but because they're the key to eternal life with Him.

Intrigued but need to know more? I had lots of questions myself. Check out the web page listed in the resources section at the end of this chapter. It does a beautiful job of explaining eternal salvation through Jesus Christ.

This isn't the last we'll be seeing of Jesus Messiah in this study. He takes a prominent place at the book's end, kind of like a grand finale in the fireworks show.

In a fireworks show, the comet, the willow, and the strobe rockets are all impressive. But when we stretch out on the hood of the car and gaze into the night sky, what we're really there for is the perfectly orchestrated program at the end, the one that overwhelms us with emotion until it's leaking from our eyes. The one that resonates in our chests and makes us clap and cheer.

That's Jesus in Obadiah. Who am I kidding. That's Jesus everywhere.

Person the Second

It's all downhill from meeting Messiah, Lord of Creation, God of the Universe. Although, thinking strictly in human terms, meeting a prophet is up there, too.

Have you met one before? Me neither. Well, there were times as a kid I *thought* my dad was a prophet (when he warned I'd feel keen regret if I "kept it up"), but apart from that, I've never had the privilege.

That makes today super special. The prophet I want to introduce you to is right over here...

Hey, Obadiah! I'd like you to meet someone. She's read your stuff and has been wanting to go deeper. Like, really understand it.

Lovely reader friend, meet Obadiah, the man of the study. His Hebrew name means "servant of Yahweh," and he's definitely lived up to it. As you know, he's also got a rather sweet publishing credit. In his role as servant of God, he wrote twenty-one verses of Scripture that have been touching hearts for eons.

Aaaaand, that's where the official Obadiah meet-and-greet ends.

I wish I could give you a proper introduction. You know, tell you his lineage, where he was born, what else he did with his life. Shoot, I wish I could tell you the years he was alive. I mean, I can take an educated guess on the century, but no one knows with certainty where to place him on a timeline (the next chapter's topic).

His personal information has baffled scholars for millennia. All we're given about him is one introductory phrase: "The vision of Obadiah." Given so little, the best we can do is list the twelve other Obadiahs named in the Old Testament (don't worry, I'll spare you the full list) and wonder which one he might be. If any.

Among the Old Testament's Obadiahs, we find a variety of men. There's a descendant of Saul as well as a descendant of David through Solomon. Another is one of David's thirty "mighty men," warriors renowned as fierce and efficient fighters.

In 1 Chronicles 9, there's a Levite and a returned exile, both with the same name. Still another is named in Nehemiah as one of those who sealed the covenant. While reading 1 Kings 18, I was convinced that the Obadiah who protected the 100 prophets from Ahab had to be the book's writer. He just seemed the type to write an inflammatory message to the enemy. You know, the bold and faithful type, a bona fide servant of God. Alas, the timeline makes it improbable.

We *do* know it was written in Hebrew, and since the Edomites spoke a different language, we can confidently say the Jews were the book's audience.

"Wait, wait, wait," you might be thinking. "I've read the book, and almost the entire passage is addressed directly to the Edomites, so how can the Jews be its audience?"

Great observation, chickee. If you'll put a pin in it, we'll come back to that when we discuss verses 2–4. It'll be worth the wait.

There might be few biographical facts about the author we can point to definitively, but the letter's style and content give us a little more. They allow us to glean other details about him. For example, because of Obadiah's emphasis on Jerusalem, we can presume he lived there or at least made his home in the southern kingdom of Judah.

As far as style, Bishop Lowest, "the great master of Hebrew criticism" (according to John Calvin), stated that Obadiah "left but a small monument of his genius."[1] He's referring to Obadiah's poetic talent. The Bible Project calls the book "a series of divine poems."[2]

The brainy people with theology degrees tell us most of the book is written in poetic form (with some prose at the end), although it's hard to tell in English. Obadiah was a skilled writer. His voice is clear and animated, and he uses literary devices such as imagery, parallelism, rhetorical questions, and irony. Even in English, that talent comes through, so I imagine the Hebrew version would be pretty sweet reading for the linguistics experts in the crowd.

That's all the information about the writer gathered over the centuries. It's not much, I know. But hopefully, it's enough to sketch a rough picture of our guy and set you up for the rest of the study. In the next chapter, we'll do our best to put him on a timeline and align him and his book with world events.

Pop Quiz:

1. How much do you know about Obadiah?
    A. So much. I could write this study.
    B. Obadiah is a minor prophet in the Old Testament. He prophesies minorly and probably says some good stuff I should know.
    C. Is he that one guy in the Bible who helped that one king that one time? Or...hmm... Wait. Did he write a book of the Bible?
    D. Oba-who?

2. What is your relationship with Jesus Christ?
    A. We're old acquaintances. We talk long distance every day, but there's always more to know about Him. A girl can't get too close to Jesus.
    B. I met Jesus a while ago, but we've lost touch. He keeps reaching out, but then a

butterfly flutters past, ya know? Life is busy, but I'm going to make more of an effort. Starting now.

C. Jesus is my new best friend. This study might be a little more than I'm used to at this point in my spiritual walk, but I'm going to give it my best.

D. I don't know Jesus yet, but I'm interested. The links below might answer some of my questions.

Resources:

God's Plan of Salvation:
https://bible.org/article/gods-plan-salvation

3

Timeline Talk

The vision of Obadiah. Thus saith the Lord God ...
Obadiah 1a

This is the part in the study where I'm supposed to attach a timeline on a corkboard and definitively drive a tack into the span of years Obadiah lived. I really wish I could.

We'll blame Obadiah's single-mindedness. God gave him a vision, and he wrote the vision. Not one word more, not one word less. True to his name, he is the very definition of *servant*. We can add *selfless* to that, too, because as we already covered, he left us nothing about himself. Nothing.

> The vision of Obadiah. Thus saith the
> Lord God concerning Edom.
> (Obadiah 1a)

That compels us to look to the text for clues about the year, but because the events described in the book can be interpreted a couple different ways, we still fumble around for an absolute date. For Obadiah and anyone living at or around his time, the passage would have made perfect sense, but for those of us looking back on centuries and centuries of strife between Edom and Judah, it's not as clear.

The two nations were at each other's throats for a thousand years, and the Bible records several major clashes between them. So, which one is Obadiah talking about? That's the question of the hour (or centuries).

There are two main camps in the discussion. Some scholars point to the year 587 BC during Jerusalem's fall to the Babylonians under Nebuchadnezzar. Others move the dial further back on the timeline and place Obadiah at 845 BC during Jehoram's reign.

During the earlier era (Jehoram's), Edom had been under Judean control since the year King David subdued them. Tired of all that, they "revolted from under the hand of Judah, and made a king over themselves" (2 Kings 8:20). If you're like me, despite a lifetime of Bible study, the revolt during Jehoram's reign rings zero bells. The Babylonian captivity is much more familiar, but even in that, I could use a refresher.

In exploring our two options further, we'll start with the 845 BC Obadiah Timeline possibility and Edom's revolt under King Jehoram. If you're trying to remember whether Jehoram goes on the list of good kings or evil kings, think evil. Definitely evil. (You know you're wicked when you're compared to Ahab.)

Jehoram had "forsaken the Lord God of his fathers. Moreover he made high places in the mountains of Judah and caused the inhabitants of Jerusalem to commit fornication, and compelled Judah thereto" (2 Chron. 21:10–11). Because of his wicked ways, a plague struck his household, and three neighboring kingdoms were "stirred up against Jehoram," the Edomites, the Philistines, and the Arabians (2 Chron. 21:16).

For our alternate Obadiah Timeline option, fast forward 240 years. We'll stop first at 605 BC and the Babylonians' first invasion and deportation of Judeans.

Quick recap. During this time, Daniel (of lion's den fame) was among those taken into captivity and hauled off to Babylonia (Dan. 1). Over the next nineteen years, Hebrew kings still sat on Judah's throne, and godly prophets still prophesied, including Jeremiah and Ezekiel.

During those same years, several other attacks and deportations occurred until, finally, in 587, the Babylonians struck their final blow and utterly destroyed Jerusalem, including Solomon's Temple. Edom was involved in that humiliating takedown.

So, those are the two possible events Obadiah references: 845 and Edom's revolt under Jehoram or 587 and Edom's involvement in Judah's destruction. Some scholars and pastors are so set in their stance they won't even provide the alternate view, but it's only fair you're presented with both options here:

Arguments for earlier King Jehoram date (845):
- Obadiah doesn't mention *total* destruction of Jerusalem.
- No mention the burning of the Temple.
- No mention of Nebuchadnezzar.
- Nebuchadnezzar wouldn't have "cast lots" (v. 11) for Jerusalem; he was too greedy to divide the spoils.

Arguments for later Babylonian siege date (587):
- Obadiah speaks of "captivity" (v. 11–12).
- He also speaks of "total destruction" (12).
- "Foreigners" are mentioned, implying Babylonians in addition to the Edomites (11).

You'll notice that those who go with the 845 option mostly base their position on what they *don't* find in the book. An argument from *silence* will never be as strong as an argument from evidence that is *present*. Were the Judeans taken captive during the Babylonian invasion? Yes. Was Jerusalem totally destroyed? Yes (2 Kings 25; Jer. 6; 52).

To the last point made in favor of the 845 date, Obadiah's parallel passage (Ezekiel 35) also doesn't mention Nebuchadnezzar or Babylon, but no one questions whether the prophet is speaking of that era.

For these reasons, and because most scholars lean this way, we'll be using the Babylonian date during this study, but if you want to investigate these positions more thoroughly, I encourage you to do so! Bible.org does a fabulous job of laying out both sides in a neutral manner (link provided in the resources section below).

It's always good to have a general understanding of the arguments and answers (that's why we're here, right?), but the *what* of the book is far more important than the *when*. Even so, it's helpful to us visual girls to see the events laid out on a neat line, so I've provided one at the chapter's end.[1]

For this study, these are the dates to remember:

587 BC	Jerusalem falls to Babylon
588–550 BC	Writing of Obadiah
551 BC	Edom falls to Babylon

As you can see, according to this Babylonian-Era Timeline, Obadiah wrote his oracle sometime between the fall of Judah and the fall of Edom. In a nutshell, the Edomites assisted the Babylonians in 587 and, per Obadiah's prophecy, paid for it in 551 when Babylon turned on Edom.

There's *so much* to say about those two dreadful battles (and we will), but unless we understand exactly who these Edomites were and why they did what they did, we can't fully appreciate their actions or the Jews' reactions to them.

That's why over the next few chapters, we'll talk about Edom's backstory, then its terrain, culture, religion, livelihood, and history. Knowing these ancient people on such an intimate level will provide unique insights into the verses we'll be studying.

Buckle up! It's gonna be great.

Pop Quiz:

1. We can be absolutely, positively certain what year Obadiah was written.
   True / False
2. Which biblical event is April basing this study on as the one central to Obadiah's writing?
   a. 845 BC Jehoram's shenanigans
   b. 587 BC Babylon's invasion
   c. 612 BC Assyria's downfall

Resources:

The timeline section of the following web page is a quick read. If you have a few minutes, do check it out: https://bible.org/seriespage/4-obadiah.

A BRIEF HISTORY OF EDOM AND ITS INTERACTIONS WITH ISRAEL

Note: most dates are estimates

2000 B.C.
Birth of Jacob and Esau

1400 B.C.
Edom refuses passage of the Children of Israel through their land.

1000 B.C.
David brings Edomites under subjection

800s B.C.
Edom throws off Judean oppression and sets up kings.

586 B.C.
Jerusalem falls to Babylon with Edom's aid

587-550 B.C.
Writing of Obadiah

551 B.C.
Edom falls to Babylon

300s B.C.
Edomites named Idumeans

129 B.C.
John Hyrcanus compels Idumeans to merge with Israel.

37 B.C.
Herod becomes King of Israel

1970s A.D.
Busayra, Edom's capital, excavated

4

Ambassador's Announcement

The vision of Obadiah. Thus saith the Lord
God concerning Edom; We have heard a
rumour from the Lord, and an ambassador is
sent among the heathen, Arise ye, and let us
rise up against her in battle.
Obadiah 1

Are you ready for this? All buckled in? Way to be a
rule follower. Before we hit the gas and head into
Scripture, here are a few insider tips to set you up
for success:

1. Although there are other outside players, the
two most pertinent characters in this book are
Edom and Judah.

2. Throughout the book, the terms "Esau" and
"Teman" (the name of Esau's grandson, listed as a
duke in Gen. 36:15) are used as different names
for Edom; and "Jacob," "Jerusalem," and "Mount
Zion" all refer to Israel.

3. We'll be taking the first sixteen verses in
chronological order. Ancient Hebrew authors

often disregarded writing events as they happened sequentially, a technique Obadiah uses. If we reorder his verses, we can line them up with the history we'll cover. Here's the new arrangement: 1, 10a–14, 2–4, 5–9, 10b, 15–16, 17–21. Don't worry. We'll put them back when we're through. All right, ladies, flip to Obadiah verse one. Let's get cracking.

Obadiah must have been an introvert. In the first twenty words, he gives God the credit three times for what he's about to say. Directing the spotlight off himself, he labels the message a vision, which is a message understood to be from God. Next, he pulls out that familiar prophety phrase "thus saith the Lord God," which tells us he's reporting God's words, and just in case anyone is unclear about the source, he then says the rumor (or report) that's circulating is "from the Lord."

Who is this "we" receiving the report, you ask? Well, it's not God and some other unnamed party. Here, God is dictating to Obadiah, telling him to write about himself and others who've heard the rumor.

So who else heard? It's been suggested that a group of prophets all got the same message and interpretation. Could the other prophets have been Jeremiah and Ezekiel, Obadiah's contemporaries?

Later in the study, we'll read similar messages of judgment from both those prophets. So, yes, it's possible the "we" here means Jeremiah and Ezekiel and possibly others whose messages weren't recorded. Urijah, for example, was a prophet we know next to nothing about, but he's a contemporary of Jeremiah and named as faithful to Yahweh (Jer. 25:20–23).

Other translations of the Bible use modern punctuation we more readily understand. The New King James Version puts the prophet's "we" aside in parenthesis.

> The vision of Obadiah. Thus says the Lord God concerning Edom, (We have heard a report from the Lord, And a messenger has been sent among the nations, saying, "Arise, and let us rise up against her for battle")

The ESV uses an additional colon at the front end.

> Thus says the Lord God concerning Edom: We have heard a report from the Lord, and a messenger has been sent among the nations: "Rise up! Let us rise against her for battle!"

I like it. The extra punctuation visibly distinguishes the introductory phrase from God's decree concerning Edom.

Also interesting here, this is both a physical report from the realm of international politics and a spiritual report (vision) from God. In the very literal sense, a "messenger has been sent among the nations." Some believe this to be an angel sent by God to stir up the nations against Edom.

Others take it to mean an actual ambassador (of the human variety) had been sent out by the king of one nation with the task of ordering other nations to join him in battle. Either way, the message comes from God. Whether angel or man is being used as a mouthpiece, it's God's order that's circulating.

Be careful here not to confuse the KJV word *rumors* with how we define the word today. This wasn't gossip or unsubstantiated chatter picked up from back alleys or trade routes. The Hebrew word for "rumor" used in the third line is closely associated with *announcement* or *news*.[1] In other words, a deliberate message from an individual.

Babylon was the big dog in the region at the time, although not for much longer. The message given to a human ambassador would have been from the last king before the empire's fall, King Nabonidus (r. 556–539 BC). He would have been responding to some unacceptable action on Edom's part.

Want to hear how I think it went down? Sure, you do.

1. God sends an angel to whisper orders into Nabonidus's ear.
2. Nabonidus instructs his scribe to pen the battle summons on a scroll. "Rise up!" he writes. "Let us rise against [Edom] for battle!"
3. Nabonidus seals it with his fancy red wax and his fancy gold ring, gives it to an envoy, and sends him off with a kick to the pants (because he's a meany like that).

That might be my overactive imagination at play, but it does align with how God works, using earthly kings to advance His eternal plan. As the proverb says, "The king's heart is in the hand of the Lord, as the rivers of water: he turneth it whithersoever he will" (Prov. 21:1).

Whatever the actual story, we know three things for certain—surrounding kingdoms were intentionally riled up against Edom, God is the instigator, and Edom had better duck and run.

This is a great reminder that God is the master behind every human world event. Nothing happens without His hand directing it behind the scenes. Keep that in mind as we watch the world around us fall apart. There is a greater script being read from Heaven, folks, and its ending has an HEA (happily ever after).

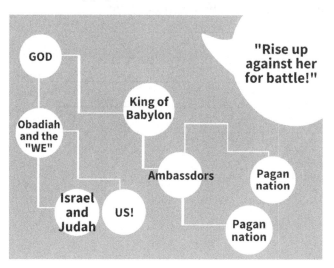

Let's sum this up, shall we? The report of Obadiah verse 1 came in the form of a vision from God, who'd given it to Babylon's king, who then gave it to ambassadors, who were sent to spread it among pagan nations. He also let Obadiah and the "we" in on the plan. All clear?

Yeah, okay, that was a bit confusing. Let's put it another way. See above for a visual. Better? I do love a good flow chart.[2]

Now that the *how* of the message has been settled, we'll move on to the *who* of it.

Introducing Edom…

Pop Quiz:

Can you think of a few other memorable "thus saith the Lord" passages? Write the references here. Feel free to use ye old Google.

_____

_____

_____

_____

_____

5

Introducing Edom

Thus saith the Lord God concerning Edom.
Obadiah 1a

There's something about Edom that fascinates me, and I'm not quite sure what it is. Maybe it's the kingdom's complicated history, which we'll talk about later in the study. It could also be that I never gave Edom much thought before this deep dive into Obadiah. Up to now, the Edomites were just one more of the pagan "-ites" that harassed the Jews throughout the Old Testament.

Ammonites, Hittites, Canaanites, Amalekites, Vegemites. Okay, maybe not that last one. Granted, the Israelites (more -ites!) harassed them back, but you see what I mean. They all blur together, right? So, learning about Edom now, really grappling with who they were, how they lived, and where they disappeared to, has opened an exciting window to the Bible I never knew existed.

Since I was attending church before my umbilical cord fell off, I often tease that I was born on a church pew. When you've been studying something for so long, you begin to feel like there's nothing left to learn, which is silly. God always has something to teach us. Regardless, it's where the brain goes. That might be the reason I'm always digging, digging, going deeper into definitions, implied meanings, and like now, the kingdoms surrounding the Promised Land, specifically Edom.

Do you like geography? I do! God does too because He uses it in Obadiah to both condemn the Edomites for their arrogance and to prove His Word is Truth. That's why, in this chapter, we're going to talk a little about their livelihood and the rugged landscape they pridefully called home.

Boots on, everyone, we're going mountain climbing.

Nest Among the Stars

Roll out the maps, geography nerds! Spin the globe! Power up Google Earth!

For the rest of you (yes, you in the back having high school PTSD), there's a basic map included below. Also, deep breaths. There's no pop quiz over this and no odious group projects.

We're all smart girls and can read a map, so I won't go into descriptions of Edom's borders except to say that it was located in modern-day southern Jordan on the southeast corner of the current State of Israel. But certain things can't truly be appreciated on a map, such as elevation and topography.

You can't see the red sandstone Edom was named for. You can't hear the eagles screeching overhead. You can't feel the sting of the desert heat slapping your cheeks or the steep, rocky terrain crumbling beneath your sandals. And "rocky terrain" is putting it mildly.

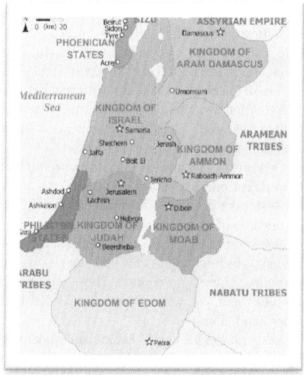

Kingdoms of the Levant, 9th century BC[1]
Attribution: By Oldtidens

Edom enjoyed a strip of fertile land on the lower elevations where a small population existed, but the Edomites who made it onto the pages of Scripture were the hardy folk who lived on the mountains. If you've conjured an image of Heidi in the Alps, wandering grassy slopes with baaing sheep, nix it. Think more Frodo climbing Mount Mordor. Barren rock. Steep cliffs. Plunging ravines.

That's Mount Seir. And the Edomites lived on the loftiest peaks. They cut their houses into the rock and lived on the edges of cliffs. In some places, their territory rose to 5,700 feet. Their western edge was broken up with ravines and cliffs that fell away to a dry, rocky valley[2] (today's Wadi of Araba). Glad I recommended those mountain shoes?

It's safe to say, any invading army would have its work cut out. My imagination takes me to the old westerns where the Native Americans dig into the crevices of a canyon and fire arrows down on naive invading American soldiers as they traipse through, feeling confident in their superior weaponry. There's no contest. Those who live in the rocks and know their passageways have the upper hand, literally.

Busayra, the Edomites' capital and only major city, was located on the crest of a mountain ridge. Surrounded on three sides by deep ravines, it was their only fortified city.[3] Edom was never more than a loose confederation of tribes, many of them pastoral, and that was only in their later years.

Any power they had did not lay in their military, but in their inaccessible mountain.[4]

Grape Gatherers, Copper Smelters, Toll Takers

Time to come down from the highlands to that fertile strip I mentioned earlier, although "fertile" here is a relative term. The desert did provide some pasture for the nomadic herds, but if the annual precipitation of ancient Edom was anything like modern southern Jordan, they received less than four inches a year.[5]

The rains were seasonal, too, coming in floods. No dummies, those who lived in the lower levels of the kingdom built terraces to control the flow of rainwater and allow them to grow gardens. Figs and grapes did particularly well, and Edom became known as prolific cultivators of both.

One other product they exploited was copper. They mined, smelted, and transported it extensively all through the Iron Age (1200–500 BC). Their smelting technology was quite advanced, almost modern in its methods of using flues and air-channels,[6] The industry brought much-needed income to this semi-nomadic kingdom of tribal shepherds, but it also made their region highly desirable to surrounding kingdoms, including those as far south as Egypt.

Their other main source of income was through tolls. They controlled routes leading from Arabia and the Dead Sea into Damascus, Gaza, and the Mediterranean.[7] A fellow didn't enter their territory uninvited, and those who did go through paid hefty fees for the privilege. Most of the towns in the lower elevations, carryovers from nomadic days, were not fortified with enclosing walls, and even though most of the agricultural production took place there, the heartland of the kingdom, the capital, was in the heights.

Changing Political Borders

Sunday school review! Remember the United Kingdom of Israel? To set the stage for our study of Obadiah, that's where we're headed. It's our first stop, anyway. By the end of this chapter, we'll cross Judah's southeast border into territory that's less likely to be found in a church Sunday school curriculum—Edom.

Israel's monarchy began under Saul. King David expanded the kingdom's territory through endless battles, and his son Solomon built the Temple and enriched the kingdom and his own personal wealth until he "surpassed all the kings of the earth in riches and wisdom" (1 Kings 10:23). Both David and Solomon, though flawed, did right in the sight of the Lord. Their progeny? Not so much.

In the mid-900s BC, after King Solomon's death, the kingdom of Israel divided into Israel in the north under Jeroboam, and Judah in the south under Rehoboam. There comes a host of spiritual reasons for this, but politically, the northern tribes were disgruntled over heavy taxes levied on them (1 Kings 12:16–19). It always comes down to money, doesn't it?

So there they were, two kingdoms with a shared history but an increasingly disparate view of God. Meaning, Israel made its own gods and danced to its own spiritual tune, while Judah waffled back and forth between worshipping the One True God and the gods of surrounding nations. Because of Israel's spiritual rebellion (and dismissal of repeated warnings from prophets), over the next four hundred years this happened:

- Assyria invaded and subjugated Israel (721 BC).
- God saw King Hezekiah's faithfulness and spared Jerusalem from invasion (2 Chron. 32).
- Babylonia and Media conquered Assyria, taking Israel and Judah with it (626 BC).

There's always a bigger fish, y'all.

To put things into perspective, Babylonia controlled all of modern-day Iraq, Syria, Jordan, Lebanon, Israel, and parts of Saudi Arabia and Turkey.

Some of the cities and kingdoms under Babylon's thumb were allowed to go about their business if they paid tribute and didn't plot behind closed doors. Other kingdoms got flattened and were forced to live under Babylonian "satraps" or governors.

Israel fell under the second category, but she had fallen to the Assyrians two hundred-plus years earlier and had been kingless ever since (thanks a lot, kings who did evil in the sight of the Lord).

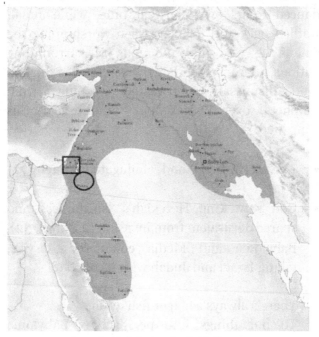

Neo-Babylonia at Its Height[8]
☐ - Judah
○ - Edom
Attribution: Neo-Babylonian

To the south, Judah had a few godly kings, such as Hezekiah and Josiah, so God gave them a few more years to enjoy their autonomy. Even so, they were subject to Babylonian authority and weren't spared the occasional assault and deportation of captives (shoutout to Daniel and Ezekiel).

We've finally arrived at 587 BC and the infamous devastation of Jerusalem and destruction of the Temple. This was Judah's big fall. Again, kudos to evil kings whose blatant rebellion removed God's blessing from the kingdom.

That's what Israel and Judah were up to in the mid-500s BC. Meanwhile, Edom dodged the Babylonian bullet, er, spear and managed to avoid plundering and captivity. Her puppet kings were answerable to Babylon, but they were allowed to continue governing their traditional territory, all contingent on regularly delivered tributes. Nebuchadnezzar couldn't build his Hanging Gardens on pennies.

In a couple of chapters, we'll go deeper into Edom's fascinating history and learn why exactly they deserved the judgment detailed in Obadiah. For now, because a little backstory always helps, we're going to rewind the sundial all the way back to 2000 BC and a very pregnant woman who's resting in her tent, swollen feet propped up, begging God for an answer.

Pop Quiz:

1. Before picking up this book, how much did you know about Edom?

    A. I knew Edomites were descended from Esau. (They both start with an E, so duh.) I also knew they were a thorn in Israel's side. Weren't all the -ites?

    B. I knew the name Edom, knew it was a pagan nation, knew it was probably on God's naughty list. Outside of that, I got nothin'.

    C. Nope. Never heard of them. I'm a clean slate. Fill me in!

2. Edom, which means red, was named for its abundant sandstone. What else was Edom named for? Rather, *who*...?

Answer: _____

Go deeper with *But in Mount Zion*:
- Read "You Are a Player."
- Quote: Are you stamping yourself onto His mission or are you stamping *Him* into it? Are you stepping into the spotlight or stepping out of the way so others can see the Light?

Part 2

THE
BOOK'S
ORIGIN
STORY

6

The Troublesome Twins

...your brother Jacob...
Obadiah 10a

This chapter begins a new section of our study. A very important one, since understanding a character's backstory is pivotal to appreciating a plot, and these two characters have quite the backstory.

The spat between neighbors Edom and Judah didn't start over who hogged the best parking spot or whose dog left a gift on the lawn. Their troubles go way-way back to a set of twins we all know.

Because I need my outline fix, here's what we have ahead in this new section.

2. Book's Origin Story (verse 10a)
   a. Jacob and Esau, the twins who started it all
   b. Thefts, blessings, and threats
   c. Esau's "blessing" fulfilled in Edom

Time to hop in our way-way back time machine for a trip to the year 2000 BC (more or less) and the tent of "your brother Jacob," the *your* in this case being a direct address. Obadiah is speaking to Edom in verse ten.

Three times in the book, our prophet uses the term "Jacob" or "house of Jacob." These aren't casual genealogical mentions. They are inserted to heighten Edom's guilt and shed full light on their offense against Judah. More on that later. For now, know that Obadiah is pointing to Edom and Judah's shared heritage. Once upon a time, their ties were pretty tight—family doesn't get much closer than twins.

If you've been in church any amount of time, you've heard the account of Isaac and Rebekah's twin boys, Jacob and Esau (Gen. 25–33). By the story's end, Jacob is the star of the show, the hero who overthrows his shortcomings and completes his story arc with a nail-biting climax and satisfactory resolution, but what about Esau?

He should get an award, too, for playing the sympathetic villain; although, *villain* isn't a perfect description of him. He does oppose his brother, even threatening to kill him, but he's also the antihero of his own story. Just as Jacob is the father of the future kingdom of Israel, so Esau is the origin of his own nation. Pretty heroic, that. At least as far as the Edomites are concerned.

To them, he would have been Father Esau, revered patriarch of old, the ancestor whose closest kin betrayed him, stole from him, denied him familial and divine blessing. To them, he was the redheaded stepchild (literally/not literally) who overcame it all and built a nation from the crumbs of his inheritance.

But I'm getting a wee bit ahead of myself. The twins' backstory might be an unfamiliar account to some of us, and to those who call it old news, let me ask you: have you ever read the story from Esau's perspective? Have you ever considered it from the angle that every struggle with the Edomites stemmed from those few chapters in Genesis?

I haven't either. How about we remedy that?

The Twins' Pre-birth Prophecy

The brothers' story begins where everyone's does—in the womb. But of the countless billions of us who've taken that journey, only a handful can claim a prophecy spoken about them before they saw the light of day. Off the top of my head, I'm thinking of Sampson, Samuel, John the Baptizer, and the Star of the show, Jesus. There are probably more, but whatever the number is, it's small.

The common denominator between them all is their vital roles in the setting God placed them in. Samson was a warrior, judge, and liberator. Samuel was a prophet, priest, judge, and military leader. Both men are listed in the Bible's so-called hall of faith (Heb. 11:32). John heralded the Messiah's arrival and was instrumental in instituting the church's ordinence of baptism. And Jesus, well, He *is* the Messiah.

That's quite a distinguished list to be included in and not a grouping we usually consider: Jesus and Esau. But as Jesus can be considered the second Adam, He might also be considered the second Esau. Hold that thought.

God felt both of Rebekah's twins were significant enough to His eternal plan to merit the same pre-birth treatment as some of the greatest figures in biblical history. These boys are significant. *Both of them.*

They not only received a prophecy straight from the mouth of Yahweh, but they got the ignoble distinction of pre-birth brawling. Those of us with siblings have plenty of experience with squabbles (that red Cabbage Patch stamp was *mine,* Sister), but how many can say they've been fighting since *the womb*? At least two. These boys. And it didn't stop for a long, long time. Almost their whole lives.

Can you imagine the strain on Rebekah? From chapter one. No, from the prequel, she sported those exhausted-mom bags under her eyes.

Every pregnant mother has her concerns. If there isn't enough movement, she worries the baby isn't okay. If there's too much movement, she worries her kidneys are not okay. I'm sure mothers of twins have twice the fears. All you moms out there who've carried twins (or more) can chime in and let us know if you ever worried about your babies *fighting* while you were pregnant. I mean, is that a thing?

Rebekah was so concerned, she took it to God. "She said, 'If it be so, why am I thus?' And she went to enquire of the Lord" (Gen. 25:22).

Enter: the pre-birth prophecy.

"And the Lord said unto her, Two nations are in thy womb, and two manner of people shall be separated from thy bowels; and the one people shall be stronger than the other people; and the elder shall serve the younger" (Gen. 25:23).

Whoa. The older serve the younger? That ain't right. Not according to their tradition of birthright. That's what I would have been thinking if I were in Rebekah's sandals. Imagine having to tell the menfolk the news. "So, uh, Isaac honey… good news, bad news. Which do you want first?"

Imagine the disappointment to learn your boys were probably going to hate each other. It was almost inevitable with how God said it would all play out.

Esau was born first, and true to their quarreling nature, Jacob came out right on his heels. Literally. As the Scripture says, "And after that came his brother out, and his hand took hold on Esau's heel" (Gen. 25:26). Right out of the gate, Jacob makes good on the prophecy. While causing his mother extreme agony.

An arm-first birth is another way these boys were not natural. Today, limb presentation in delivery calls for an emergency C-section, since the baby is at high risk of getting stuck in the mother's pelvis. But thousands of years ago? Unless angels swooped down to administer an epidural, Rebekah pushed that child out on a shrill scream.

Her own survival was probably in question too. Yahweh had said nothing of *her* in the prophecy, whether she'd be around to watch them grow up to hate each other. She was certain both her boys would live, but in a situation like this, her life was not assured.

In a sense, the angels did swoop in. That she lived through the birth was miraculous. Makes you wonder if that experience had something to do with her favoritism. In time, her "boys grew: and Esau was a cunning hunter, a man of the field; and Jacob was a plain man, dwelling in tents. And Isaac loved Esau, because he did eat of his venison: but Rebekah loved Jacob" (Gen. 25:27–28). It's not unusual to feel a closer bond with one child than another, but Isaac and Rebekah took it to an extreme, which had to have aided the rift between their sons.

We aren't told why Rebekah loved Jacob more, but they went through a major ordeal together. Could her bond with Jacob have stemmed from his status as a miracle baby? Who knows.

Clearly, the way to Isaac's heart was through his stomach. He and Esau had that in common—food ranked rather high on their priority list. High enough for Esau to exchange his birthright for a bowl of red stew when he came in from the field famished.

The Twins' Birthright Exchange

That's right, exchange. A single bowl of stew for the honor of being head of the home. There was no theft here, not yet. Here's the account straight from Genesis.

And Jacob sod pottage: and Esau came from the field, and he was faint: And Esau said to Jacob, Feed me, I pray thee, with that same red pottage; for I am faint: therefore was his name called Edom. And Jacob said, Sell me this day thy birthright. And Esau said, Behold, I am at the point to die: and what profit shall this birthright do to me? And Jacob said, Swear to me this day; and he sware unto him: and he sold his birthright unto Jacob. Then Jacob gave Esau bread and pottage of lentiles; and he did eat and drink, and rose up, and went his way: thus Esau despised his birthright. (Gen. 25:29–34)

First off, who does that? Who holds food over the head of a dying man to use as leverage to get the thing he wants? Especially a brother. A *twin*. That was a real jerk move on Jacob's part.

Second, this sounds like a serious case of hangry or whatever irrational condition sets in when a person is beyond hungry. Whichever it was, Esau's growling stomach set the twins' lifelong argument into irrevocable motion. It converted that continually looming threat into reality.

The verse says he "despised his birthright," a heart condition that didn't blossom overnight. This event was merely the tangible fruit of an outlook that was years in the making.

According to Merriam-Webster.com, to despise means "to regard as negligible, worthless, or distasteful."[1] This suggests he didn't take his duties as firstborn seriously, and since Isaac was no spring chicken when the boys were born (sixty), Esau was probably at least partly running the place early on in his life. Yet here we see him throwing away that privilege for a bowl of stew as if looking for any excuse to be rid of responsibility. Why would he do that?

Maybe he was crabby because there was talk that God didn't want him for the position of head of household. If that was the case, I can sympathize. It would take a mighty humble soul to swallow that bitter pill. Maybe his parents never told him of the prophecy, and he simply had no interest in being the man of the house. The outcome was the same—he ditched his birthright and, in so doing, flicked the first domino in a long series of pre-ordained events.

It's early days here in chapter 25, and already the picture being painted of Esau isn't pretty. If I were using a flannel graph to tell this story, the background felt would not be the happy, happy rainbow scene. It would be the one with the black thunderheads reserved for Noah and Jonah.

Moving on to the birthright thing. So...what is it anyway? The word birthright stands for all the privileges and advantages a firstborn son received. This man received a double portion of his father's inheritance so he could care for any unmarried sisters, widows, or children in his family unit.

He also became the priest of the family, responsible for offering sacrifices at appropriate times (Job 1:5). Finally, he inherited judicial authority, which meant he punished the wayward and blessed the obedient (Gen. 28; Num. 3:12–13; Deut. 21:15–17; 2 Chron. 21:3).

The position of firstborn or first-begotten was a sacred role that (brace for goosebumps) was perfectly fulfilled by Christ the Messiah, who is the firstborn of God, of the Church, of the world, and of the dead (Rom. 8:29; Col. 1:18; Heb. 1:4–6). He received a double portion of His Father's inheritance when He was given Heaven's throne and (one day) will reign over all the Earth. It's with that inheritance that He provides for us, His children. He is also the Great High Priest whose mercy allows us to approach the Throne (Heb. 4:14–16).

Finally, Jesus is our faithful and true Judge. "For the Father judgeth no man, but hath committed all judgment unto the Son" (John 5:22). His children must all, one day, stand before Him "that every one may receive the things done in his body, according to that he hath done, whether it be good or bad" (2 Cor. 5:10).

Esau squandered his birthright, but God's promises cannot be undone by man. To Abraham, the Almighty said, "And in thy seed, shall *all the nations* of the earth be blessed" (Gen. 22:18, italics mine). Messiah might have come through Jacob's blessed line, but "as many as received [Jesus], to them gave he power to become the sons of God, even to them that believe on his name" (John 1:12). What Jacob and Esau screwed up, Jesus set to rights. Where Esau despised his birthright, Jesus embraced and perfected His, granting salvation to all. To me, to you. To all the nations.

Chills, amiright? At times, to our human thinking, the Bible seems to be a jumbled-up ball of string with hundreds of threads twisting together but having nothing to do with each other. Then we come across a truth like this, and we're reminded that even when the Bible seems like one of those complex knots that we can't make heads or tails of, it actually has order and purpose and holds everything together. Like the manrope knot or the albright knot. Or the knot you tie when you get married. (On second thought, that last one is closer to the yarn the cat got into.) I digress.

Okay, we've got Esau fed and Jacob smugly birthrighted. What next? Right, the boys get hitched.

Esau's Unwise Marriages

There weren't a lot of church-bred girls around Jacob and Esau's part of the world, so finding a godly woman couldn't have been easy. They were all idol this, idol that.

But did Esau even *try* to find one who pleased God? Doesn't seem that way. There's no mention of Esau seeking Yahweh's guiding hand when he chose his two Hittite brides.

There is, however, mention of how they "were a grief of mind unto Isaac and to Rebekah" (Gen. 26:35). Later, "Rebekah said to Isaac, 'I am weary of my life because of the daughters of Heth: if Jacob take a wife of the daughters of Heth, such as these which are of the daughters of the land, what good shall my life do me?'" (Gen. 27:46). I'm no perfect daughter-in-law, but I don't think I've ever driven my MIL to contemplate the purpose of living. How about you? Maybe don't answer that question.

There is some serious family drama going on here, y'all. And it all began with two selfish boys fighting over womb space. It's always the little stuff that causes the biggest rifts. From arguing over stew to relinquishing birthrights to marrying women outside the faith.

So what spiritual beliefs did his wives probably hold? The Hittites engaged in a highly developed polytheistic religious structure. A little insight into their system points to similarities with what will later become Edom's gods. How about some compare and contrast? We'll start with Edom.

Because of the Edomite's shared heritage with Israel, it's possible they worshipped Yahweh at the outset. Esau would have been the most likely candidate to continue his father's religious traditions. But over time, as often happens with those who don't keep a firm eye on God, the Edomites made their own version of Yahweh, reducing Him to a three-horned patron deity and calling him Qos.

Qos, whose name means "bow" (as in a stick with a pointy end, not obeisance), was considered an object of worship as a mountain god and a storm god[2] Contrast that with Yahweh, who is known as the Everything God. He isn't the sun god or the death god or the god of battles or harvests. He is *all* those things and everything else our fragile human minds can think up, and then some. He is the great and mighty I AM (Exod. 3:14), and Qos is a pitiful wannabe.

And yet, Esau's descendants chose Qos over Yahweh. They "changed the glory of the uncorruptible God into an image made like to corruptible man, and to birds, and four-footed beasts, and creeping things... [and] changed the truth of God into a lie, and worshipped and served the creature more than the Creator, who is blessed for ever. Amen" (Rom. 1:23, 25).

In this passage, Paul points to how the Edomites could have devolved from worshipping the One True God to their own adulterated version, the one seen on the next page. Keep this image of Qos in mind as we move on to the Hittites.

As mentioned, Isaac and Rebekah's Hittite neighbors worshipped a multitude of deities (depending on the town and ethnic group), but there's also evidence in archaeology of mountain cults, which considered certain mountains to be gods. They also had a key divine family, a god and goddess with a child. The male was a weather god who bestowed fertility through rain. He had different aspects, two of which were "weather god of the thunder" and "weather god of the lightning." Sounding similar yet? It gets better.

Reliefs found at Aladjahüyük, an ancient Hittite settlement in Asia Minor, show the weather god in the form of a bull. The bull was the weather god's sacred animal because the bull is strong, loud, and fertile. But the bull wasn't only a symbol of the weather god, it was an anthropomorphic representation of the god himself.[4]

How about another look at Qos, the Edomites' patron deity? Do those horns look vaguely bullish to you? Yeah, me too.

Why am I making such a big deal about this? Because the Hittites and their religion were well established by the time Esau's children could be called a kingdom with a patron deity, so any similarities between them probably went from Hittite to Edomite, not the other way around. Do you think it's possible Esau's wives brought their religious practices with them and that they stuck? Could be.

Attribution: Edomite_Goddess[3]

Isn't that how it happens? You look away from Yahweh for a minute because that other thing is *so shiny* *insert giant singing crab.* Before you know it, you're bowing down to mountains. Or to stone heads rocking a sweet set of horns. Or your kingdom's divine family.

Or your nine-to-five. Or your beauty, reputation, or bank account. Or whatever *shiny* thing you've set up in your heart in place of Him.

All it takes is one step away from the true God. The next one comes so much easier.

Also, don't marry a Hittite. Sound wisdom there. Take it from Rebekah, the disgruntled mother-in-law.

Jacob's Much Wiser Marriage

In contrast, our hero Jacob returned to "the house of Bethuel," his mother's people, to find a wife. He went on orders from his father, and as a reward for his obedience, he received his father's blessing as well as God's.

It was during that trip when Yahweh visited him in a dream (Gen. 28). This is a pivotal moment in Jacob's life, the "crossing the threshold" of his hero's journey. If he were Frodo, he'd be packing his bag to embark on his adventure. If he were Luke Skywalker, he'd be standing over his aunt and uncle's graves, ready to leave Tatooine. Both of these characters have "met the mentor" (Gandalf/Obi-wan), had a revelation, and committed to the journey.

Bethel is that place for Jacob. It's where God reveals Himself as the quintessential mentor. This is where Jacob stops reacting to life, stops compliantly obeying his father's directives, and starts following Yahweh. In verse 18, when Jacob sets up that stone as a pillar, he's taking decisive action. He's putting his old life behind him and moving forward with new purpose and under new management.

We're never shown Esau pursuing Yahweh, not once. He seeks other things like food, revenge, and even reconciliation with his brother, but if he seeks the God of his father, we aren't shown it. It's an auspicious start for his one-day nation.

Not that it's an excuse for poor choices and rejecting Yahweh, but Esau *did* have it rough from the get-go. There was the whole heel-grabbing incident, plus the prophecy that basically said he wasn't good enough to be a clan leader. And we can't forget the stew-birthright kerfuffle.

Then came Jacob's infamous theft of Esau's blessing in Genesis 27. That passage, the completion of the prophecy, calls for a Bible study book all on its own. I encourage you to pause here and read that chapter start to finish even if you're familiar with the story. Take special note of *all* the players in the deception, because that's where we'll be going next.

Seatwork:

Jacob and Esau received a prophecy before they were even born. Here are two others we haven't mentioned who claim that God's purpose for them began in the womb. Find these two verses and write them here.

Jeremiah 1:5

_____

_____

_____

_____

_____

Isaiah 49:1

_____

_____

_____

_____

_____

What does this pattern of God's attention to
womb babies tell you about human pre-birth
value?

_____

_____

_____

_____

7

Parental Peccancies

...the elder shall serve the younger.
Genesis 25:23b

In reading Genesis 27, did you pay special attention to each family member's part in Jacob's theft of Esau's blessing? That's the drama we're heading into now, starting with Isaac's parental peccancy.

What, you don't like the word peccancy? Aw, come on. Work with me here. The thesaurus wasn't offering much in the alliteration department for words meaning "fault" or "offense." Which is what Isaac and Rebekah had in spades in this blessing-theft episode.

In direct violation of the prophecy given to his wife, Isaac states in Genesis 27:1–5 that he would declare Esau his heir and bless him as such. He then gives his son directives on how the occasion will proceed. Talk about raising cain. Especially when the wife hears of it.

There's a ton to unpack in this passage, but we'll stick to the questions pertinent to our study of Esau: what exactly is this blessing Isaac wants to give, and why would he bless his *eldest*?

First, this was no trite after-sneeze "bless you." It wasn't even on the level of Jesus's greatly loved "beatitudes" (Matt. 5). No, this blessing was in a class all its own. Yahweh first gave it to Isaac's father in what we now call the Abrahamic Covenant (Gen. 12:1–3; 15).

After Abraham died, God blessed Isaac, too. Isaac was aware that at some point, true to Yahweh's pattern, the blessing that both he and his father received would be passed along to his offspring. This blessing thing was a big deal. They all knew it. Even Esau, who had so blithely tossed aside his birthright.

They were also likely aware of the oracle given to Rebekah when she was pregnant. You know the one where Yahweh said the "older shall serve the younger"? Yeah, that one. Soooo, what's Isaac doing here? Why is he moving to make Esau head of the household, even in light of the prophecy and Esau's own "despising" of his birthright?

Isaac either didn't understand the prophecy or didn't care. The Bible gives no guidance on that. But we can safely assume he was fully aware of it. His wife did not keep the oracle from him.

Considering all the rivalry between Rebekah/Jacob and Isaac/Esau, it's hard to imagine she wouldn't use the prophecy as ammunition to advance her favorite, which had the inevitable consequence of feeding the rivalry.

Their family counselor would call this a toxic cycle.

It's worth taking the time to pause here and backtrack to review each of Abraham and Isaac's blessings. You'll find them in Genesis 12:1–3 and 25:11. Give them a quick read.

Okay, did you notice the common element between them? Hint, it has to do with timing.

There's little to nothing given on the wording of the blessing Isaac received, but we can glean one simple, yet impactful, detail—God was the one who blessed him. He also blessed Abraham. In His own perfect time, God used His own mouth to bless both Abraham and Isaac.

Do you think it's possible He had intended to speak Jacob's blessing as well? Maybe when his father died as He'd done before with Isaac?

We can't know, because Isaac took the task upon himself. Verse 1 makes it clear *he* called Esau to him so that he could bless him. Why? Because God told him to? If He did, Scripture doesn't let us in on it.

The reasoning Isaac gives for beginning this process is that he was old and blind and feared his days were numbered (27:1). He was *afraid,* he said. (Spoiler alert: he lived another forty years.) If Isaac was afraid of anything it was that his number-one kid would not receive the blessing.

Check out the wording of the Genesis 27 blessing, then contrast it against the oracle given to Rebekah. As you read, remember that Isaac meant the blessing for *Esau.*

Blessing spoken to Jacob: "<u>Let people serve thee</u>, and <u>nations bow down to thee</u>: be <u>lord over thy brethren</u>, and <u>let thy mother's sons bow down to thee</u>: cursed be every one that curseth thee, and blessed be he that blesseth thee" (Gen. 27:29).

Prophecy given to Rebekah: "Two nations are in thy womb, and two manner of people shall be separated from thy bowels; and the one people shall be stronger than the other people; and the elder shall serve the younger" (Gen. 25:23).

Do you see the inversion? The prophecy stipulates Esau would serve Jacob, but in the blessing, Isaac says the exact opposite in four distinct phrases. I underlined them. Kind of hard for the older to serve the younger if the younger is the one doing the bowing.

Also, notice that he phrases it in a general way (using "brethren" and "mother's sons") that includes not just Jacob but all his descendants and any other children Rebekah might have. Can a guy be more contradictory to God's Word?

We can only guess at Isaac's motives or understanding of the oracle. There's no way of knowing his heart or even his level of mental acuity. His body held out another forty years, but maybe his mind wasn't keeping pace.

We could speculate all day, but there's no doubt that, over the course of his boys' lives, Isaac had plenty of opportunity to properly search out Yahweh's will regarding the matter. Instead, he chose his own wisdom, much as his sons did at various stages of their lives.

Fortunately, by Genesis 28, Isaac has gotten his act together. In the first four verses of the chapter, he sends Jacob off to Padanaram to find a wife, blessing his youngest properly as *himself* before sending him off.

> And God Almighty bless thee, and make thee fruitful, and multiply thee, that thou mayest be a multitude of people; And give thee the blessing of Abraham, to thee, and to thy seed with thee; that thou mayest inherit the land wherein thou art a stranger, which God gave unto Abraham. (Gen. 28:3–4)

Redemption is available for all. And despite all the drama and human bungling of the blessing, Isaac still made it into the Hall of Faith. In Hebrews 11:20, Isaac is mentioned as a man of exemplary faith because he "blessed Jacob and Esau concerning things to come."

He might have messed up the timing and the twin, but he got one thing right—the faith. The boy who trusted his father and laid down on the altar (Gen. 22) is the same man who trusted his Father to bless his sons.

Isaac wasn't the only peccant parent in this situation. In verses 6–17, Rebekah, who got wind of the impending blessing, panicked, and concocted a convoluted scheme for her son to deceive her husband. "Now therefore, my son, obey my voice according to what I command you," she said.

The plot? Jacob would dress up like his twin and receive the blessing in his stead. His blind father wouldn't know the difference, or so they hoped. It's the original parent trap (without technicolor). Although, the goat-hair arms were about as ridiculous as some of the antics the movie twins got up to.

My preemie son came out covered in a fine fuzz. Hairy babies are a thing, but they almost always lose the hair as they grow. Apparently, Esau was the exception to the rule and kept his "garment" through to adulthood. It would certainly make impersonating him difficult, but the cunning Rebekah pulled it off.

Actually, she pulled off three peccadillos here. The first was toward her husband, whom she made to look weak and foolish. The second was toward Jacob, because she was the little devil on his shoulder, luring him into sin. The last, toward Esau, might be the most grievous. Of all the men in her family, Esau had the most tenuous relationship with the God who hadn't chosen him as leader even though in human thinking he deserved it.

Did Rebekah care about trying to reconcile her son to her family and to Yahweh? We see no indication of it. And for a mother to take such callous action, it couldn't have been the first time she'd behaved so contrary to Esau's benefit. This is most likely a consequence of many years of development of a scornful attitude toward her eldest.

It's easy to believe this sort of treatment might have been what led Esau to choose wives from such a vastly different belief system. The faith he'd grown up with hadn't done him too many favors. Neither had his mother.

In this one act, Rebekah might have completely obliterated whatever relationship she could have had with her eldest son. Shockingly, she was so sold on this multi-layered deception, she was willing to be cursed for it. Which makes me wonder... Did she feel she had some sort of spiritual get-out-of-jail-free card? Did she believe she was acting as God's vessel? He *had* spoken an oracle to her many years before, and it *was* (from all appearances) about to go belly up.

So, she meddled. Instead of letting God Almighty do His own work, she stuck her nose in the middle of things. She either forgot or disregarded Yahweh's mandate to Abraham (et al.) to walk blamelessly before Him. Cutting her own trail, she conveniently set aside the fact that *He* would fulfill the covenant (Gen. 17:1).

In this family of four, no member gets off scot-free before God. If we place their individual offenses on a human scale of "badness," Esau comes out the lightweight. In chapter 8, we'll see how.

Seatwork:

It's in a mother's nature to fix, whether it's her toddler's untied shoes or her grown son's wayward lifestyle. One of the trickiest parts of the job is keeping her role and God's role in their appropriate slots. To all the mothers in the audience, what are you sticking your nose in that God has labeled as His? What situation are you manipulating to serve your purpose?

8

Supplanter and Sobber

He cried with a great and exceeding bitter cry.
Genesis 27:34

Isaac and Rebekah, through manipulation and deception, have their demerits on the chalkboard, but what about their boys? We're most familiar with Jacob's sins in this account. He's often called the supplanter or the deceiver, and for good reason. He superseded Yahweh's timing and took what wasn't his to take.

When Rebekah laid out her plan to Jacob in verses 5–10, he did hesitate, but not because he believed what they were doing was wrong. He was afraid if their little trick went splat, he would be cursed instead of blessed.

After his mother assured him she would take upon herself whatever curse might come of it, he embraced her scheme to hoodwink his father (such a gentleman). He really gets into character, too, going so far as to credit God for the hunt's success. That was lie number four, so he'd already gotten into the groove.

Jacob seemed to be a compulsive liar. (I've seen his yearbook. He was voted least likely to become a real boy.) He fibs so many times in this episode, it's hard to keep track. Not counting the deceptions of wearing his brother's clothes and the goat fur he uses to make his hands hairy, he verbally lies six times. And it works.

His father, though dubious at first, kisses him, smells the field on his clothes, and blesses him. Score! I wonder though. How triumphant did Jacob feel at his success? When did the guilt set in? Did it at all? If it didn't in this moment, maybe it did when he heard his brother sobbing.

Speaking of the brother... Esau, who likes to play the victim here, was all thumbs-up about taking a blessing he knew no longer belonged to him. When reality comes home to roost and the consequences start falling into place, he's a different guy.

In verses 30–40, we watch Esau fall apart as he receives the punishment for despising his birthright and, as a result, the blessing that came with it. Oh, these boys. These fractious, quarrelsome boys. If only they'd tried harder to get along. If only the one hadn't been so insistent that red rubber stamp was his. Maybe if they'd put more effort into their relationship, they wouldn't have gotten to this point.

Trouble in the family rarely starts with a shotgun blast or a prophecy of doom straight from Yahweh's mouth. Its origins are usually of the poke-poke variety. A cruel tease, a streak of jealousy, an unrepentant harsh word. The author of Hebrews uses Esau as a cautionary tale, warning us to keep the peace, so we don't end up crying over whatever scraps are left to us.

> Follow peace with all men, and holiness, without which no man shall see the Lord: Looking diligently lest any man fail of the grace of God; lest any root of bitterness springing up trouble you, and thereby many be defiled; Lest there be any fornicator, or profane person, as Esau, who for one morsel of meat sold his birthright. For ye know how that afterward, when he would have inherited the blessing, he was rejected: for he found no place of repentance, though he sought it carefully with tears. (Heb. 12:14–17)

The "it" Esau sought with tears was the blessing, not repentance. Esau does not "say sorry" in this chapter, but he does boo-hoo. "And when Esau heard the words of his father, he cried with a great and exceeding bitter cry, and said unto his father, Bless me, even me also, O my father" (Gen. 27:34). He desperately wished to undo what had happened, but it was too late. The NIV phrases that last line this way: "Even though he sought the blessing with tears, he could not change what he had done."

A cold, cold heart would have to be sitting in a person's chest to not sympathize with his predicament. The descriptions of his reaction make it impossible not to put yourself in his place and feel the knife of disappointment and betrayal.

After a bout of anger, followed by his father's refusal to reverse the blessing, Esau tries again. "Hast thou not reserved a blessing for me? And Esau said unto his father, Hast thou but one blessing, my father? Bless me, even me also, O my father. And Esau lifted up his voice, and wept" (Gen. 27:36b, 38). I envision a man on his knees, tears streaming into his beard, face planted in the dirt as he wails. "Is there no crumb of blessing left for me?" Little good it did.

Long-due regret has finally come around for a slap in Esau's face. Did he even consider this result back when he was weighing the pros and cons of stew versus birthright? Since he didn't, his only recourse here was to beg for a show of mercy.

He does that, but he directs his pleas to the wrong father. As King David would later do, Esau should have lifted his face to Heaven and cried, "Be merciful unto me, O God, be merciful unto me: for my soul trusteth in thee: yea, in the shadow of thy wings will I make my refuge, until these calamities be overpast. I will cry unto God most high; unto God that performeth all things for me" (Ps. 57:1–2).

Esau never displayed the wisdom of his twin's progeny, David. He and his descendants never looked to God to solve their problems or fulfill their purpose. Continually carving out their own way, they refused to live in subjection to Yahweh, dragging out that sin as far as the Early Christian Church.

To be fair, that's the pattern for each actor in this Genesis episode, but Esau is particularly good at despising the sacred. He ditched his birthright for a bowl of stew, and in his plea to his father, he behaved as if the blessing Jacob received were one of many, instead of a "one of one."

Isaac didn't turn a deaf ear to Esau's crying. (No surprise—Esau was his star child.) But he was limited in what he could grant his eldest. The blessing he gave to Jacob consisted of temporal possessions ("fatness of the earth...grain and wine") and a spiritual possession with Yahweh as its true source. The Almighty had guided Isaac as he voiced the blessing. Consequently, there was only *one* to give out. Jacob had received that blessing, and Isaac had no authority to revoke it.

In later chapters, the study will walk us through both boys' blessings unfolding and fulfillment, some in part and some in whole. But next, we'll pick apart Esau's blessing to lay groundwork for our study of Obadiah's message to his descendants.

Seatwork:

Feeling extra studious? Read both Esau's blessing (Gen. 27:39–40) and Obadiah 1–21 and note any phrases or verses you think connect the two.

9

Blessing-Curse-Prophecy

Bless me, even me also, O my father...
Genesis 27:38

Isaac did grant Esau the thing he begged for, but the "blessing" Esau received could easily be taken as a sort of curse, which indicates Yahweh was the guiding hand behind its creation. Would Isaac willingly curse his pet son? Me thinks not.

He would have done everything in his power to advance his favored son despite the setback, but no one is fooled, especially not Esau. The man is already crying, so to be nice, we'll call Isaac's speech a prophecy instead of a curse.

The second half of it is easy enough to pick apart. The first bit, not so much. To help us along, we'll return to the original Hebrew. Don't worry, I'll keep it light! No glazed-over eyes allowed.

Before we go there, keep in mind that Isaac *cannot* duplicate Jacob's blessing. This is important. He cannot give both sons "the fatness of the earth" and the "dew of heaven," even though it might seem like that's exactly what he's done.

There's only *one* eldest-son blessing to be had, remember, which was the whole reason for all the sneaking around. It also means there must be another interpretation to Esau's prophecy, a subtler one. Wouldn't you know, there is? And it's pretty cool. Some might call it poetic. In the prophecy, Yahweh (through Isaac) is playing off the expressions used in Jacob's blessing by inverting them.

For reasons I haven't discovered, some of our older English versions of Isaac's first line use a variation of the phrase "*shall be of* the fatness of the earth" and "*and of* the dew of heaven." The Hebrew phrase יִ_ּ_מַ_שְׁ_מִ (miš·man·nê), however, is more properly translated "away from," the entire phrase being "*away from* the richness." The next line borrows the same structure לְ_טַ_מֻּ (ū·miṭ·ṭal), meaning "*away from* the dew."[1]

Have a look at the lines in the King James Version:

> And Isaac his father answered and said unto him, Behold, thy dwelling shall be the fatness of the earth, and of the dew of heaven from above; and by thy sword shalt thou live, and shalt serve thy brother; and it shall come to pass when thou shalt have the dominion, that thou shalt break his yoke from off thy neck. (Gen. 27:39–40)

Look again, this time at a literal translation from Hebrew:[2]

> His father Isaac answered him: "Behold, your dwelling place shall be away from the richness of the land, and away from the dew of heaven above. You shall live by the sword, And serve your brother, But when you rebel, you will tear his yoke from your neck." (Gen. 27:39–40)

In short, Esau and his children were destined to live *away from* verdant land. Within short order, that was exactly where they were.

The region of Edom had fertile plains, but as stated, it was most notable for its rugged desert landscape. German explorer Ulrich Jasper Seetzen (1767–1811) called it "the most desolate and barren mountains probably in the world."[3] Not a pretty picture, and they didn't choose it themselves. In fulfillment of the prophecy, Yahweh gave Esau that land (Deut. 2:5). This wasn't a promising start to that second nation promised to Rebekah's womb.

Even so, by the time the twins reconciled, Esau seemed to be prospering. In Genesis 33:9, shortly after the brothers hugged it out, Esau turned down Jacob's livestock peace offerings by saying, "I have enough, my brother; keep that thou hast unto thyself." Either he'd really found prosperity in Edom, or he was "all hat and no cattle" as we say in Texas. Yeehaw. Basically, too proud to admit life stinks.

It's a possibility, but I don't think that was the case. The Bible's description of how he received his brother is too genuine, even if it is hard to imagine a guy could be content with a ginormous piece of rock for a home. Or that he could make anything of it.

But that's exactly what the Edomites did. They settled nicely into their no-fatness, no-dew home. Put up their picket fence. Hung out the shingle. Angled the recliner just so in front of the TV. According to Scripture, they were a proud people and fought fiercely for their territory, taking extreme measures centuries later to retain it (more on this later). Which is another aspect of the blessing-curse-prophecy, right? It stated, "You shall live by the sword."

Roman historian Flavius Josephus defines the Idumeans (a future name for the Edomites) as "a tumultuous and disorderly nation, always on the watch on every motion, delighting in mutations."[4] Throughout Scripture, they are known for their pride, treachery, greed, and violence (2 Chron. 10:11, 25:14–24; Jer. 49:16; Amos 1:9, 11; Obad. 3). In fact, those very things—acted out against Jacob's descendants—were what prompted God's ultimate condemnation and the writing of Obadiah.

The next stipulation of the prophecy, "[You shall] serve your brother," is played out over the following centuries. Genesis 33 records a tissue-worthy reconciliation between the twins, but there was no getting away from any of the three prophecies: Rebekah's, Jacob's, Esau's. To silence any doubters, they all say the same thing. Esau will serve Jacob.

In no time flat, the oracle attached to their birth was fulfilled, and two nations developed. Esau became Edom. Jacob became Israel. Per Yahweh's word, the relationship between them was one of constant and cyclical servitude, rebellion, and renewed subjugation.

Edom started out independent, an extension of that hard-won harmony between the twins. There must have been residual bitterness though, because when the nation of Israel returned to their Promised Land (Canaan) from a long, back-breaking stint in Egypt, Edom refused the Children of Israel passage through their country (Num. 20).

Here, I'd like to set a backdrop on this episode by giving insight on Yahweh's position on Edom shortly before their insult to Israel. During the wandering years in the desert, when God was establishing the guidelines for the Israelites' proper worship, He made special mention of the Edomites in a command to the Israelites, saying, "Thou shalt not abhor an Edomite; for he is thy brother" (Deut. 23:7). Whatever His people's attitude toward Edom, Yahweh considered them brothers and wished Israel to do so, as well.

Edom must not have gotten the memo because at their first opportunity to establish friendly relations (and potential allies) with their soon-to-be neighbors, they deliberately snubbed them.

The book of Exodus, as well as Egyptian records, confirm that by that time, 400+ years after Jacob's children moved to Egypt (thirteenth century BC), Esau's descendants were firmly established in Edom.

The area southeast of the Dead Sea belonged to them and was also the path Israel needed to take to get to their home country. Edom's refusal to let them pass from Kadesh en route to Canaan cocked the pistol for centuries of conflict. Guided by Yahweh, the Hebrews didn't battle for the right but bowed to Edom's demands and went the long way around. Israel might not have raised arms, but they never forgot. Neither did Yahweh.

Before long, Israel's first king, Saul, defeated the Edomites (1 Sam. 14:47), then David, their second king, had the delightful task of bringing them under Israelite governance (2 Sam. 8:14). They attempted a revolt during Solomon's reign (1 Kings 11:14) but failed and remained under the Israelites' thumb until the time of King Jehoram when they rebelled again.

On and on it went. Rebellion. Battle. Reconquest. Despite this constant strife, which God could not have approved, we are told of His continuing mercy in Deuteronomy 23:7. "Thou shalt not abhor an Edomite; for he is thy brother: thou shalt not abhor an Egyptian; because thou wast a stranger in his land."

Kings Amaziah, Uzziah, and Jotham were also forced to deal with their ancient brother-nation (2 Kings 14:7, 22; 2 Chron. 25:11, 26:2). Finally, the time came for the last line of the prophecy to be fulfilled. "And it shall come to pass, when you become restless, That you shall break his yoke from your neck" (Gen. 27:40).

And so they did. During the reign of King Ahaz, Edom shook off their overlords for good (2 Kings 16:6; 2 Chron. 28:17). At this point, Israel had long been a divided kingdom, each under Assyrian and then Babylonian authority. In God's timing, they each fell into captivity, while Edom remained an independent kingdom. But that wasn't to last either.

Because Obadiah.

Yahweh always gets the last word. We'll go into Edom's downfall in a later section, but for now, I want to hammer in the final nail of Edom's coffin. Long after Babylon's crushing blow to both Israel and Edom, the twins' descendants were still duking it out.

Josephus's history states that around 129 BC, John Hyrcanus, a Hasmonean leader and Jewish high priest, dealt the final blow. Hyrcanus forced the Edomites to incorporate into the Jewish state[4]—the ultimate "serve your brother." From there, in fulfillment of yet another prophecy (Obadiah, Obadiah!), Edom disappears off the pages of history, becoming only a region that the Greeks called Idumea.

So, that's the blessing-prophecy-curse handled, as well as its fulfillment. In a later chapter, the study will go deeper into the fulfillment part, but for best comprehension of Obadiah, it's important to create a solid mental picture the history between Edom and Israel.

Soon, we'll see how the story of Edom goes full circle, from the blessing-curse-prophecy of Genesis through the condemnation of Obadiah and finishing in historical fulfillment.

I hope all this background into Jacob and Esau has been as informative and interesting to you as it is to me. Even now, as I review it for the umpteenth time for clarity, I can't help the excitement bubbling up over how seamlessly the Bible zippers together. But instead of having two chains of teeth that fasten, it has countless.

What's extra cool is that the zippers are the almost-invisible kind you'll find on fancier clothes. No one sees the thing that's holding the dress together. No one even thinks about the tool that's keeping it all from falling apart.

It isn't until we start tugging on the pull-tab and studying the teeth that we see it and understand how important it is, how many interlocking parts it has, how complex it is, and how perfectly all the pieces fit together. The zippers not only fit together with each other but, like eternity's most perfect cog-and-wheel system, every verse fits into history.

Which is where we're going next. History! But not Edom's. They get a break for a minute. Judah is our next destination.

Seatwork:

At the study's end, in "Edom Through the Ages," I've written out every reference to Edom and Idumea in the Bible coupled with a brief description of what's going on in the passage.

For an aerial view, I've created a (more or less) chronological list of Scripture covering those events. You'll find the list, "Edom's Interactions with Israel," free to download on my website at link below. Glance over the bullet points or read the verses in full. Either way, I think you'll come away with a stronger sense of Edom's role throughout the biblical ages.

www.aprilgardner.com/fireandflame-freebies

Go deeper with *But in Mount Zion*:

- Read "A Blessing on Your Head."
- Quote: In Scripture, the "destiny," or blessings, God chooses to pour out on certain people ... are powerful and enduring, truly irresistible courses of events that fulfill a great purpose. Who were those people? Abraham for starters, then Isaac, followed by his twin sons, Jacob and Esau. ...portions of their blessings endure to this day. How does any of this apply to us? In this section of the study, we'll cover that.

Part 3

EDOM'S
VIOLENCE
against JUDAH

10

Tumbling Temple

*For thy violence against thy brother Jacob
shame shall cover thee.*
Obadiah 10

This is the point in the study where things get ugly. Like, blobfish, naked mole rat, aye-aye ugly. Google them. I'll wait.

Okay, are you tracking with me now? We're talking sad, sad times here. Of our story's twins, Jacob is going down first, followed in short order by Esau. Momma told you boys to quit fighting. Now, the Father has to step in.

I jest. Sort of. While Judah did indeed squabble endlessly with Edom, the truth is God allowed her destruction and captivity because of her sin against *Him*, not Edom. However, Edom fell strictly because of her violence against Yahweh's Chosen People. But I get ahead of myself.

Ten chapters into this study, we've covered quite a bit of terrain, having enjoyed a thorough introduction to Obadiah and its setting, become acquainted with Edom, and taken a whirlwind tour through the characters and prophecies that started it all.

Good job, us. We are now all geared up to start picking Obadiah apart. As we do, we'll be stepping back (sometimes, *way* back) to view each verse from every angle—from the perspective of Obadiah's past, from his present, and from both his and our future.

As a refresher, here's what's still ahead:

3. Edom's violence against Judah
    a. Judah's downfall (10a)
    b. Edom's hand in it (11–14)
    c. Ezekiel and Jeremiah weigh in
4. Edom's violence repaid
    a. Arrogance and foolish boasting (2–4)
    b. Wrath prophesied (5–7)
    c. Wrath played out (8–9, 10b, 15–16)
5. Judah's ultimate victory
    a. Three blessings (17–18)
    b. Three promises (17–18)
    c. Jesus Messiah will reign (19–21)

In earlier chapters, we discussed Obadiah verse 1, using it as an introduction to the book and the study. From here out, it'll be like the game Fruit Basket Turnover. Time to shake these twenty-one verses out of their spots and rearrange them according to history's timeline, which means we're now skipping ahead nine verses.

> For thy violence against thy brother Jacob
> shame shall cover thee.
> (Obadiah 10)

What's this violence Obadiah is talking about? The threats Esau made against Jacob's life? The scuffle they had over that red rubber stamp, I mean, er, Yahweh's blessing? That could certainly be alluded to here, as could any number of instances over the 1,000 years of strife between the brother nations. But the offense the author points to here is much more recent.

It's also the book's big question, the one we considered in chapter two, "Timeline Talk." Our two main options were Edom's rebellion against King Jehoram or Edom's part in Babylon's sacking of Jerusalem almost three hundred years later. As you know, we're going with the later event in this study, so let's talk about that, shall we?

Before we get into Edom's destruction as prophesied in Obadiah 2–9, which is bad enough, we need to go down the more tragic road of Judah's downfall. Why more tragic? All life has value, right? Yep. But I place the greater weight of tragedy on Judah because 1) they're God's Chosen and 2) Solomon's Temple went down with them.

The Temple's collapse marks the end of an era and the beginning of a much less pleasant one. Yahweh, as well as His people, must have been deeply grieved to watch the Holy Temple burn at the hand of the "uncircumcised."

The cause of all this destruction? Rebellion, plain and simple. Refusal to submit to God's way instead of their own. So much death. So very avoidable.

From here to the end of the chapter, we'll recount how the sacking played out and start our investigation into Edom's betrayal.

If you're like me, Babylonia's invasion and captivity of Judah has always been a vague mental image of fire and rubble, screaming and running, chains and cattle prods, despondent Judeans trudging off to Babylon to become miserable slaves. Okay, admittedly, that's kinda vivid and detailed (the inside of my head is a lively place), but what about the particulars of how it all went down? How exactly did the once-glorious kingdom of Judah fall so hard?

As with every major historical event, there's way more involved than we'll ever know, but there *are* some details we can determine by piecing together verses of Scripture. Other things can't be called fact per se, but they lean strongly toward certain conclusions. All it takes is a little investigative research. Pull out your magnifying glasses and houndstooth caps, girls. We're going sleuthing.

Unfortunately, the scope of this study doesn't allow for all the backstory into how Judah found itself in such a position of weakness, but we can conjecture about why Babylon decided to attack. This wasn't the first incursion. They'd already struck several times over the decades, but this time, they went for the throat.

Why? What changed? I mean, Judah and Babylon seemed to have a working relationship there for a while. Apart from two to three raids, Babylon ruled from afar, letting Judah do her thing so long as she sent regular tribute and didn't revolt. So, what went wrong?

I'll give you three guesses.

1. A goodhearted Judean vigilante ambushed wagons heaped with gold on the way to King Nebuchadnezzar's coffers and redistributed it to the poor. Old Nebby, who'd really, really wanted that gold to add begonias to his Hanging Gardens, got his pants in a twist and sucked his thumb until his troops marched off to set Jerusalem ablaze.

2. In Jerusalem, Judah's king hosted a meeting with representatives of the local Big Six—Edom, Moab, Ammon, Tyre, Judah, and Sidon—and hatched a plot to stand up to Babylon. A prophet showed up and said, "Break up the party, boys. You're already doomed." They did, but King Nebby got wind of it anyway. The rest is history.

3. Edom skipped off to Babylon to tattle on their brother-kingdom, whining, "That red Cabbage Patch stamp was *mine*. Make them give it back." King Nebby said, "If

you can't share, no one gets it." He then put the super cool self-inking stamp out of reach on the top of the refrigerator. Neither sibling saw it again. The battle continues to this day over who it really belonged to. No wait. That's me and my sister. My bad.

Ah-hem. Pay no attention to Option 3. Clearly, my sister and I still have some issues to work out.*
Back to business...

If you picked Option 2, you are the winner! Actually, there's a little of 3 in there, too—the part where Edom skips off to Babylon to side with them against Judah.

But wait, you might be saying, doesn't Option 2 state that Edom was at the meeting to scheme against Babylon, making them proclaimed allies? Yup. Edom had recently pulled up a chair with Judah to plot resistance against Babylon. Then suddenly, wham! A knife in Judah's back.

Starting to get a better grasp of Judah's sense of betrayal and Yahweh's wrath? Me too.

That was a bird's-eye view of events. Let's take it from the top and see if we can glean a few more details about how it all played out.

In this section, we'll cover a number of passages relating to Judah's destruction and Edom's involvement. Jeremiah, who witnessed the Temple's destruction, is probably the best place to start. It's important to note here that he wrote the book sometime between 630 and 580

BC. While we're on the subject, and since we'll be reading him next, Ezekiel's book (written 593–565 BC) overlaps Jeremiah's. These dates make Jeremiah and Ezekiel contemporaries of Obadiah.

Before those events took place, in true prophet fashion, Jeremiah warned the people to turn from their wicked ways. He also showed up at the aforementioned covert huddle of kings and gave them what-for as described in Jeremiah 27. Before we discuss that chapter, I want to point out the potentially confusing name change that happens mid-stream in verse 3 of the King James Version.

Verse one states that Jehoiakim was king of Judah. In almost the same breath, the passage switches out Jehoiakim for Zedekiah. Both are listed as the current king of Judah when Jeremiah received the message from God, which isn't possible.

Don't panic. God didn't forget who was on the Judean throne, and He certainly didn't make any mistakes. If there's an error here, it was made by a later scribe. Either that or God gave Jeremiah the message at least eleven years before the meeting took place.

But consider this. Verse 1 says, "*in the beginning of* the reign of Jehoiakim," and we know he reigned eleven years (2 Chron. 36:5), after which his son, Jeconiah, reigned for three months, *then* Zedekiah. We know Jeconiah already ruled, because the same message later states, "Nebuchadnezzar king of Babylon...carried away captive Jeconiah the son of Jehoiakim, king

105

of Judah, from Jerusalem to Babylon" (Jer. 27:20).

Such an extended gap between message-given-to-prophet and message-transmitted-to-people doesn't fit God's pattern, but who can understand the mind of God (1 Cor. 2:11)? We can't rule out the time-gap option.

The discrepancy could also be attributed to King Nebuchadnezzar changing the Judean king's name to reflect his vassal status, or it could be something else that we, in our limited human understanding, aren't grasping. Any of these options are possible. What is *not* possible is Divine error.

Since translations of the Bible into English can be a sensitive subject, I'll leave it to you to work out which position to hold. Suffice it to say, older English translations retain the discrepancy, whereas newer ones have changed Jehoiakim to Zedekiah. Hence, the potential confusion. I say all this because I'm assigning you the chapter to read, and if you're like me, reading from an older translation, you might get hung up on that name thing.

There. Got that sticky subject out of the way. Phew!

Okay, Jeremiah 27. You have your marching orders. Off you go. I'll hang out here while you read.

Oh, hey, you're back. Sorry, got distracted chasing down the foster puppy—as well as my favorite pair of flipflops. Little punk. But he repented, and the flipflop was saved. Unlike Judah, as Jeremiah so brazenly predicts.

What did you think of that chapter? Pretty bold, huh? It's an interesting read, but don't worry, we won't go through it verse by verse, á la Jacob and Esau. But real quick...

Prophets (and a bunch of other wannabes) of the false gods of the local Big Six were actively reassuring their kings that they "shall not serve the king of Babylon" (27:9, 14). They were also touting the lie that, "the vessels of the Lord's house shall now shortly be brought again from Babylon" (27:16). Those vessels had been taken in previous raids (2 Chron. 26:7). Now, the false prophets lied about their imminent return.

At the same time, Babylonia was dealing with other unruly subjects. Syria revolted in the north, and Elam attacked from the east. Internal strife kept Nebuchadnezzar's army busy at home, too. All this led to buckets of bloodshed that distracted and weakened Babylonia.[1] If the Big Six were going to stand up to their overlord, this was the time to do it. Makes sense to me.

God didn't agree. And when the Big Six, encouraged by their fibbermagoo prophets, sent ambassadors to Jerusalem to discuss gunpowder, treason, and plot, Jeremiah met them there.

In his typical no-holds-barred fashion, he told them they may as well put on chains and cattle yokes and hand themselves over because they were destined to be enslaved by Babylon—versus continue their current subjugation (Jer. 27:9–11). Some Bible commentators suggest Jeremiah, who is known for using object lessons (Jer. 19), might have shown up to the meeting with actual chains and yokes to really drive the message home (Jer. 28). That would have been quite the sight.

In whatever way he was outfitted, Jeremiah told them point-blank that God, who "made the earth, the man and the beast that are upon the ground," had already given their land away (27:5). This wasn't a new message. Zephaniah's prophecy of Judah's doom had been around since four kings back. "I will also stretch out mine hand upon Judah, and upon all the inhabitants of Jerusalem," he wrote during the reign of Josiah (Zeph. 1:4a). Now, Jeremiah urged them to "Bring [their] necks under the yoke of the king of Babylon, and serve him and his people, and live" (27:12).

They didn't. Shocker.

Well, they didn't get themselves sized for yokes or chains. They did, however, hit pause on their gunpowder plots. Whether they couldn't get along and agree on how to go about it, or they heeded God's prophet, they dissolved the parley and went home.

Phew, that was a close one. All's well that ends well, right? Not so fast, girlie.

Zip forward twenty-four chapters and a little further into that same year, the fourth of Zedekiah's reign (Jer. 51). The beginning of the end is here.

Remember that feeling you got when you were called to the principal's office, and you realized you hadn't actually gotten away with scribbling

108

"down with principal doo-doo head" on the bathroom stall? That's Zedekiah in chapter 24. In verse 59, we learn he was called to Babylon. Why? I'm sure he was asking himself that question every nail-biting mile of the way.

Many scholars believe news of that infamous Big Six meeting trickled back to King Nebuchadnezzar, who then summoned King Zedekiah to stand before him and give account of it. Having no choice but to obey, Zedekiah gathered his retinue, loaded his camels with sparkly ~~bribes~~ gifts for the king, and set out for Babylon.

And what's Jeremiah doing? Probably shaking his head in disappointment. He's also writing a letter. Actually, it's called a book (scroll), so a *long* letter. Its audience? Israelites who were already exiled there from previous deportations. Meant as encouragement, it's a message of doom for Babylon, which translates to cheer for the captives (Jer. 50:1–8).

He filled the scroll with words like, the Lord "will raise and cause to come up against Babylon an assembly of great nations from the north country: and they shall set themselves in array against her; from thence she shall be taken: their arrows shall be as of a mighty expert man; none shall return in vain. And [Babylon] shall be a spoil: all that spoil her shall be satisfied, saith the Lord" (50:9–10).

Mid-chapter pop quiz! Which kingdom ended up fulfilling this prophecy?

A. The Kingdom of Greece
B. The Kingdom of Persia
C. The Kingdom of Far Far Away

If you chose B, you get the gold star. The legendary Cyrus the Great conquered Babylon in 539 BC. That's a few decades beyond our Obadiah subject matter, but it's good to pause and reorient ourselves on the world timeline. And any opportunity to give God glory for His omniscience always gets two thumbs up.

Back to Jeremiah...

He sent this book along with Seraiah, the guy in charge of presenting royal ~~bribes~~ gifts. After reading the scroll to the people, Seraiah was to tie it to a rock and throw it into the Euphrates, saying, "Thus shall Babylon sink, and shall not rise from the evil that I will bring upon her: and they shall be weary" (51:64). Any chance this brazen prophecy didn't reach the ears of Babylon's king? Doubtful. It couldn't have helped Zedekiah's cause.

Somehow, by God's grace, Judah's king made it out of Babylon with his life. In fact, five years passed before Babylon meted out punishment. Flip forward in your Bible to Jeremiah 52. There, we read a review of Jerusalem's tragic drawn-out end. "Zedekiah rebelled against the king of Babylon. And it came to pass in the ninth year of his reign, in the tenth month, in the tenth day of the month, that Nebuchadnezzar king of Babylon came, he and all his army, against Jerusalem, and pitched against it, and built forts against it round about" (52:3b–4).

The Babylonian army besieged Jerusalem for over two years. Meanwhile, Jeremiah was in the city trying to convince King Zedekiah that if he'd only surrender the city, his family would be saved. But that would require personal sacrifice (Jer. 37–38).

Like a true narcissist, the king's reply to God's advice was, "I am afraid of the Jews that are fallen to the Chaldeans, lest they deliver me into their hand, and they mock me" (38:19). Never mind the 6,000 inhabitants of Jerusalem who'd been starving under a two-year siege.[2] Never mind the Holy Temple, which would be a lucrative target to a gold-hungry Babylonian. Never mind his own wives and children, whom Jeremiah had prophesied would be taken. No, no, better Zedekiah not be "mocked."

At one point during the siege, Egypt's army came to their aid, sending the Babylonians skittering (37:5–10). Jeremiah warned it was a temporary reprieve, and the Babylonians would be back because "though ye had smitten the whole army of the Chaldeans that fight against you, and there remained but wounded men among them, yet should they rise up every man in his tent, and burn this city with fire" (37:10). The only alternative to a torched city was for Zedekiah to give himself up.

Nope. Wasn't going to happen.

Read on through the end of Jeremiah 37 for the full account of Jerusalem's fall and Zedekiah's horrifying end.

Finished? I warned you it would get ugly. And quite dramatic, huh? Zedekiah and his head honchos sneaking out through a hole in the garden wall at night. The Chaldeans pursuing them through the plains. The Judean army scattering.

True to Jeremiah's prophecy, Zedekiah ended up in chains, which he wore to the end of his miserable days. There's no escaping God, y'all. There's no escaping sin. Hopefully, while Judah's king sat blind in his Babylonian cell, he reassessed his position with God and made some major soul adjustments.

It isn't clear whether Zedekiah ever repented, but he'd have to be atypically coldhearted not to grieve Jerusalem's destruction (Jer. 32:3–5). His tears don't show up in Scripture, but Jeremiah mourns enough for both. Lamentations 1 describes Jerusalem's physical and emotional state after Babylon finishes with them.

Halfway in, Jeremiah makes a tragic reference to yokes. Speaking as if in the voice of Jerusalem, he writes, "The yoke of my transgressions is bound by his hand: they are wreathed, and come up upon my neck: he hath made my strength to fall, the Lord hath delivered me into their hands, from whom I am not able to rise up" (Lam. 1:14). And we've come full circle.

Prophecy. Fulfilled.

Keep going in Jeremiah 52 to learn how Nebuzaradan, captain of the guard (literally translated "chief butcher/executioner") took a total of 4,600 Jews into captivity.[3] It also tells how the Babylonian army raped the Temple then burned it along with Jerusalem, tearing down every wall as they went. As we bring in other Scripture, we'll see they did not act alone.

Enter Edom, stage right.

Aaaaand PAUSE.

I know you're *totally* enthralled in the story, but this is the part where we take a bathroom break, then come back for Edom's role in the whole mess. So, run to the potty, warm up that coffee, and pull out your highlighter. We're heading in.

Seatwork:

When we read about the atrocities God allowed, we might ask, how could an almighty God stand by while so much evil unfolded? This is where faith comes in. Even when we don't understand, "His work is perfect" (Deut. 32:4). Write the verse here:

_____

_____

_____

* While I wrote this book, the 38-year squabble over the Cabbage Patch stamp came to a dramatic and unexpected end. My sister recorded it live. So who did the stamp *really* belong to? Watch the recording here:

www.aprilgardner.com/fireandflame-freebies

11

Raze It, Raze It

But thou shouldest not have...
Obadiah 12a

Obadiah 10a and 11–14 picks up where we hit the Pause button at the end of Judah's Downfall. The screen is frozen on the Temple's burning rubble. Babylonian soldiers are hacking down God's people, and Jeremiah weeps as he watches it unfold. Edom has just entered the stage and is about to reveal how vilely she can behave.

No matter how strongly we hold to our personal stances on Obadiah's place on the timeline (840s BC versus 580s BC), we must keep a question mark beside it. There's no such punctuation beside Edom's involvement in Judah's end. In a modern court of law, the kingdom would be taking a plea deal because their fingerprints are all over Jerusalem's rubble.

Scripture gives no indication of why Edom went from colluding with Zedekiah at the Big Six

Summit to acting out against Judah. Were they genuine in their original plan to revolt, or did they show up with the sole purpose of gathering intel and carrying it back to Babylon? Since Edom was under the same oppressive treatment—obligated to give a portion of the copper they mined to Babylon—it's easy to believe they did give serious thought to throwing off that burden. Especially when taking into account their own confrontation with Big Bad Babylon years later.

Then again, Judah and Edom had never been allies for more than a brief truce once every few centuries. Imagining them going into the meeting as backstabbers isn't a trial. Considering their history, Zedekiah took a huge risk giving them a place at the summit table. An opinion either way works just fine. What's clear is that Edom acted out of vengeance (Ezek. 25:12) and that, by the time it all kicked off, Edom was full-fledged Team Babylon.

Obadiah's descriptions of Edom's part in Judah's destruction are both vivid and undeniable. Psalm 137:7 also gives a startling description of Edom's battle chant the day Jerusalem burned. They're speaking of the Temple when they're quoted for saying, "Rase it, rase it, even to the foundation thereof." Can you hear Satan's voice behind that chant? Can you see him whispering into the Edomites' ears, then chortling gleefully as the Temple comes down?

When a person or people group become this blatantly anti-God, we can be pretty sure the Wicked One is behind it. Fortunately, Qos is nothing but a bull-shaped stone (Ps. 135:15–18), and El Elyon, God Most High, always gets the last word.

Verse 10 is a pivot point in the book of Obadiah. It's here that God, in concise terms, sets the crime beside the consequences. The verses leading up to this one detail the punishment, and those following detail the crime.

We'll be dealing with the verse's second half later, but it's helpful to see the whole of it now.

It's simple math.

> For thy violence against thy brother Jacob shame shall cover thee, and thou shalt be cut off for ever.
> (Obadiah 10)

Violence + Brother = Shame + Destruction

Here, in verse 10, the author puts the events in order (action, consequence), unlike in the rest of the book. Our study's structure balks against the reverse order he chose for the book, but a wise writer starts his story with an intriguing hook. In this case, it's the horror that's coming down Edom's pipeline.

Only after that grisly picture has been laid out do we allow ourselves the nagging curiosity of what in the world these Edomite guys did to deserve all that. It's a brilliant literary strategy, and I didn't even notice the events were out of order until I set about to outline this study.

So, what exactly *did* the Edomites do that's so awful? A whole list of things, starting at the top of verse 11.

While someone else did the dirty work, they stood to one side and watched (11). In Jerusalem, they observed, smug and complacent, as Judeans were literally carried away into captivity. Verse 12 accuses the Edomites of looking on Jerusalem's affliction and rejoicing over its destruction. There was a great deal of proud speak, too, boasting and mocking and all the things pompous victors say.

What were they doing in Jerusalem, anyway? It's easy to pass over that one important detail—the fact that the Edomites were *there*. They didn't

> In the day that thou stoodest on the other side, in the day that the strangers carried away captive his forces, and foreigners entered into his gates, and cast lots upon Jerusalem, even thou wast as one of them. But thou shouldest not have looked on the day of thy brother in the day that he became a stranger; neither shouldest thou have rejoiced over the children of Judah in the day of their destruction; neither shouldest thou have spoken proudly in the day of distress.
> (Obadiah 11–12)

live in Jerusalem (not in great numbers anyway, not yet), so they'd come down from their mountains and "entered into the gate of [God's] people" with the enemy for the purpose of watching their brother-kingdom fall (13).

The phrase "brother Jacob" in verse 10 is no idle addition either. God is amplifying the crime by reminding the Edomites of their shared heritage with those they've acted so vilely against. All throughout Scripture, the fact that their ancestors were brothers is never forgotten.

Violence and betrayal against family is so much more heinous than against strangers.

This betrayal can be traced *way* back. They'd wanted the Israelites gone since their Exodus from Egypt. (For review, see the chronological list of Israel's interactions with Edom [p. 98], or check out Exod. 15:15, Num. 20:14–21, and Judg. 11:17–18.) That took place in the mid-1500s BC (we'll call it 1550). It's now 587 BC. For how many generations had Edom been rubbing her hands together in anticipation of this "day of their destruction" (Obad. 13)?

According to my (ever-questionable) math skills, 964 years had passed since the Edomites

> Thou shouldest not have entered into the gate of my people in the day of their calamity; yea, thou shouldest not have looked on their affliction in the day of their calamity, nor have laid hands on their substance in the day of their calamity; Neither shouldest thou have stood in the crossway, to cut off those of his that did escape; neither shouldest thou have delivered up those of his that did remain in the day of distress.
> (Obadiah 13–14)

refused to let the "exodus-ing" Children of Israel pass through their lands. If we say twenty years make a generation, forty-eight generations of hatred were fulfilled in this event, hatred that had become "violence against thy brother" (Obad. 10).

The use of "violence" here means both literal and moral. God doesn't differentiate. "Even thou wast as one of them," He says (Obad. 11). *Them*, meaning the invaders. Whether you lift the sword or stand aside and watch it being lifted, you get labeled "violent." You also get "cut off," topped by a big bow of "shame." Happy birthday. But we'll get to the severing and shaming part a little further on in the study.

If you're on the fence about whether Edom deserved such harsh censure, move on to verse 14. Here, the Edomites go from standing in observance to cutting off the Judeans' escape to handing them over to the Babylonians. (Did you catch that authorial parallel to the evil committed against Judah? If not, it's okay. We'll come back to it.) The progression of their action is so typical of sin, isn't it?

We've all been in that place. We go down the candy aisle at Walmart to pick up a bag of mixed chocolates for the church's Fall Festival. We sneak a glance at the three-bar packs of Mr. Goodbars sitting so prettily on the second shelf from the bottom. They sweetly call our name. We subconsciously lean that way as we approach. We salivate. We negotiate. We justificate. It's been a hard week. We deserve this.

Still aiming for the mixed snack-size bags at the end, we just happen to pass the Mr. Goodbars. We glance about to make sure the kids aren't watching, then we swoop down for a snatch-and-grab. The three-pack slips into our hand, then under a box of feminine products. No one will look there.

Ask me how I know.

Hard truth here. What the eye sees, the feet approach, and what the feet approach, the hand touches. Each step in that progression is increasingly easier.

Ask the Edomites how they know.

After reading these four powerful verses (11–14), what sense do you get of the level of tragedy and destruction described? Small scale, like a house being ravaged by passing marauders? Medium scale, like a village being plowed under by the enemy as they advance their frontline? Large scale, like a key city succumbing to enemy forces?

There's some rather strong language used in the passage, words like "captivity," "affliction," "destruction," and "those of his that did remain." The last one there speaks of death and captivity so extensive it's easier to account for those who are left than for those who fell or were taken.

Other phrases aren't as on-the-nose but still give a clear indication of events. For instance, "laid hands on their substance" alludes to mass chaos and plundering, and "in the crossway" suggests those who fled were trying to run far, far away. They'd reached as far as the crossroads to another city or kingdom before being caught. Devastating, right?

Personally, in this passage, I see ruin on a national scale, like a besieged capital finally falling as a pivotal piece in a war. I see a queen toppling under checkmate. It's this description, along with the evidence of the foiled escape attempt described in Jeremiah 52 and 2 Kings 25, that leads so many to believe Obadiah was written between 587 (Judah's fall) and 553 (Edom's fall).

If an account of evil can be called beautiful, Obadiah 10–14 is it. True to his skillful literary style, the prophet depicts their actions with a certain poetic beauty.

Seven times, he says, "you should not have," (reverse Ten Commandments vibes, anyone?) and those don't even cover every transgression recorded. In summary, how about a bullet-point list of all the things? Great because, as you know, I'm a fan of information reduced to digestible phrases.

➢ Stood aside and watched captives carted off
➢ Cast lots with Babylon for plunder privileges
➢ Watched and rejoiced over the destruction
➢ Took pride in Judah's distress and bragged about it
➢ Entered the downed gates like the conquers
➢ Saw Judah's affliction and did nothing
➢ Took Judah's possessions as their own
➢ Stood in the way of victims to prevent escape
➢ Turned in those who remained (in hiding)

Anyone else feeling particularly disgusted by their behavior? Same. Knowing my flawed human nature (and my propensity for writing), if I had lived during that time, I probably would have penned a book condemning them, too.

These are the moments I have to remind myself that my sins nailed Jesus to the cross every bit as much as theirs. Even so, because of God's particular love for His Chosen People, He takes particular displeasure over Edom's actions. As we've seen, He expresses that displeasure many times in Scripture, and the finger wagging isn't restricted to Obadiah.

Coming up, we'll review what Jeremiah and Ezekiel have to say about Edom's abhorrent actions the day Jerusalem fell.

Pop Quiz:

Lots were cast seventy-seven times in the Bible for all sorts of reasons. How many instances can you name? Which is the most notable?

_____
_____
_____
_____
_____

12

Expanding Evidence

I am against thee...
Ezekiel 35:3

Needless to say, God takes issue with Edom's violence against Judah, as seen in Obadiah. There are also other passages that make specific mention of Edom's hand in Jerusalem's destruction. For a fuller picture of what went down, it's helpful to read them. Shall we give the zipper's pull-tab another tug and see what God reveals?

Recalling that Ezekiel and Jeremiah are contemporaries of Obadiah, we'll focus mainly on their version of events, starting with Ezekiel. Chapter 25 of his book makes mention of God's anger against the kingdom, but chapter 35 contains the bulk of the account.

"Behold, O mount Seir, I am against thee..." God proclaims through Ezekiel (35:3). Over the next verses, He gives the reasons He's against them, saying, "Because thou hast..."

- had a perpetual hatred, and hast shed the blood of the children of Israel by the force of the sword in the time of their calamity, in the time that their iniquity had an end (35:5)
- not hated [the shedding of] blood (35:6)
- said, "these two nations and these two countries [Israel and Judah] shall be mine, and we will possess it" (35:10)
- [had] envy which thou hast used out of thy hatred against them (35:11)
- [spoken] blasphemies...against the mountains of Israel, saying, they are laid desolate, they are given us to consume (35:12)
- rejoiced at the inheritance of the house of Israel, because it was desolate (35:15)
- appointed my land into their possession with the joy of all their heart, with despiteful minds, to cast it out for a prey (36:5)

That's quite a laundry list. Any one of those would have been enough on its own to bring down God's judgment. Combine a few of those, and you've got yourself a sure trip to the principal's office.

In Lamentations, Jeremiah's eyewitness account of Jerusalem's end brings to life Judah's futile flight for safety:

As for us, our eyes as yet failed for our vain help: in our watching we have watched for a nation that could not save us. They hunt our steps, that we cannot go in our streets: our end is near, our days are fulfilled; for our end is come.

Our persecutors are swifter than the eagles of the heaven: they pursued us upon the mountains, they laid wait for us in the wilderness. The breath of our nostrils, the anointed of the Lord, was taken in their pits, of whom we said, Under his shadow we shall live among the heathen.

Rejoice and be glad, O daughter of Edom, that dwellest in the land of Uz; the cup also shall pass through unto thee: thou shalt be drunken, and shalt make thyself naked. The punishment of thine iniquity is accomplished, O daughter of Zion; he will no more carry thee away into captivity: he will visit thine iniquity, O daughter of Edom; he will discover thy sins. (Lam. 4:17–22)

Look at all those parallels to Obadiah. How many do you count? If you need to, reread the passage with an eye to similarities between it and Obadiah. Underline each find, then consider how they connect with what we've learned already about how Jerusalem fell and how Edom was involved.

I find six specific parallels: the hunt, the eagle, the mountains and wilderness, and the mention of being drunk from the cup of wrath (implied) they'll drink.

Pretty neat, these connections, and wait until we get to Jeremiah 49. But let's cool our heels here a minute and talk about this passage.

From these verses, we can piece together that Judah either requested aid of Edom or expected it as their due. Instead, they watched in vain. Then they fled in vain.

And who exactly were they fleeing? The mentions of eagles and mountains and wilderness leads an observant girl to believe Edom herself was the one in pursuit (Obad. 3–4). Could the Judeans have fled to Edom for aid only to be chased down by those they'd hoped would save them?

I believe so, and after reading these verses, I get the sense the hunt was a lot broader in scope than I'd at first imagined. Their persecutors hunted them in the streets, in the mountains, in the wilderness. They were relentless and terrifying. There was nowhere to hide. Even the king, "the breath of [their] nostrils," could not escape.

Wait, wait, wait. Is that verse saying the Edomites were the ones who hunted down the fleeing King Zedekiah? Yep, it appears that way. They pursued and trapped "the anointed of the Lord." Zedekiah might have been an idol-worshipping coward, but he was still a prince of the House of David, anointed to the throne by the religious leaders, and sitting on it by God's allowance. Edom committed a huge no-no by capturing him.

This is a concept David understood very well. It's the whole reason he was so careful not to harm King Saul even when the man's life was his to take. "I will not put forth mine hand against my lord," he said, "for he is the Lord's anointed" (1 Sam. 24:10). If the Edomites had been reading the Histories of the Jews, they might have thought twice about laying that trap for King Zedekiah.

Admittedly, they weren't smart that way, but like every well-written villain, they were complex and exhibited a touch of conscience. We'd do well to remember that a people group shouldn't be judged lump sum, wholesale. Nations are composed of individuals, each with the opportunity to choose right over wrong, to accept or reject the One True God.

Some in Edom appear to have offered shelter to fleeing Judeans instead of turning them over for profit. Those helpful souls deserve a moment of recognition.

> Likewise when all the Jews that were in Moab, and among the Ammonites, and in Edom, and that were in all the countries, heard that the king of Babylon had left a remnant of Judah...[they] returned out of all places whither they were driven, and came to the land of Judah, to Gedaliah, unto Mizpah, and gathered wine and summer fruits very much. (Jer. 40:11–12)

Isn't it just like Yahweh to use unlikely subjects to protect His chosen remnant?

The references to the cup and becoming drunk are also curiously parallel to Obadiah's prophecy (15–16). Both of those point to principles of sowing and reaping. "Be not deceived; God is not mocked: for whatsoever a man soweth, that shall he also reap" (Gal. 6:7). Obadiah goes into this a little deeper, which we'll cover in the next chapter.

Jeremiah has a few more words to say about the whole thing, and who can blame him? Sure, his words are God-inspired, but the righteous passion behind them isn't God's alone. He shared it with Jeremiah, who was human, after all, and had personal experience with Edom's hatred.

Jerusalem burned down around the man. He might have gotten out with his life, but by the time it was over, his clothes smelled like smoke, his stomach ached from citywide starvation, his toes had mud stuck between them from being dumped into a miry well, and his head was filled with the images of carnage he would never be able to unsee. Insult to injury, the brother kingdom that Judah turned to for help, laughed in their faces, chased them down, then lit the match that finished off the Temple.

Remember that as you read Jeremiah 49:7–22, the parallel passage I promised you. For those familiar with Obadiah, it will do more than ring a bell. An entire twenty-three-bell carillon should be going off in your head.

If not, have another look at Obadiah, focusing on verses... Never mind, just read the whole book again, then see my chart here for a comparison of the passages.

Obadiah	Jeremiah
The vision of Obadiah. Thus saith the Lord God concerning Edom; We have heard a rumour from the Lord, and an ambassador is sent among the heathen, Arise ye, and let us rise up against her in battle. (1)	I have heard a rumour from the Lord, and an ambassador is sent unto the heathen, saying, Gather ye together, and come against her, and rise up to the battle. (14)
Behold, I have made thee small among the heathen: thou art greatly despised. (2) For thy violence against thy brother Jacob shame shall cover thee. (10)	For I have sworn by myself, saith the Lord, that Bozrah shall become a desolation, a reproach, a waste, and a curse; and all the cities thereof shall be perpetual wastes. For, lo, I will make thee small among the heathen, and despised among men. (13, 15)
The pride of thine heart hath deceived thee, thou that dwellest in the clefts of the rock, whose habitation is high; that saith in his heart, Who shall bring me down to the ground? Though thou exalt thyself as the eagle, and though thou set thy nest among the stars, thence will I bring thee down, saith the Lord. (3–4)	Thy terribleness hath deceived thee, and the pride of thine heart, O thou that dwellest in the clefts of the rock, that holdest the height of the hill: though thou shouldest make thy nest as high as the eagle, I will bring thee down from thence, saith the Lord. (16)
If thieves came to thee, if robbers by night, (how art thou cut off!) would they not have stolen till they had enough? (5a)	If thieves by night, they will destroy till they have enough. (9)

Obadiah	Jeremiah
If the grapegatherers came to thee, would they not leave some grapes? (5b)	If grapegatherers come to thee, would they not leave some gleaning grapes? (9)
How are the things of Esau searched out! how are his hidden things sought up! (6)	But I have made Esau bare, I have uncovered his secret places, and he shall not be able to hide himself: his seed is spoiled, and his brethren, and his neighbours, and he is not. (10)
Shall I not in that day, saith the Lord, even destroy the wise men out of Edom, and understanding out of the mount of Esau? (8)	Concerning Edom, thus saith the Lord of hosts; Is wisdom no more in Teman? is counsel perished from the prudent? is their wisdom vanished? (7)
And thou shalt be cut off for ever. (10) And they shall be as though they had not been. (16)	His seed is spoiled, and his brethren, and his neighbours, and he is not. (10)
For as ye have drunk upon my holy mountain, so shall all the heathen drink continually, yea, they shall drink, and they shall swallow down. (16)	For thus saith the Lord; Behold, they whose judgment was not to drink of the cup have assuredly drunken; and art thou he that shall altogether go unpunished? thou shalt not go unpunished, but thou shalt surely drink of it. (12)

Incredible, right? So...should Obadiah head to the principal's office, too? Plagiarism is definitely one of the "thou shalt nots" in the school handbook. Kidding! But kind of not.

Many scholars say that one of the two prophets might have taken inspiration from the other when writing his own book, but I suggest (along with a smaller voice of commentors) that both men were taking their inspiration from God, not each other (2 Tim. 3:16–17).

And we can't forget that, at the top of his book, Obadiah states something right along those lines. "We have heard a report from the Lord" (Obad. 1).

Speaking of our man Obadiah, we've arrived at his list of consequences for acting out against God's Chosen. By reading Jeremiah 49, we already touched on this, but we haven't done it full justice. In the upcoming chapter, we'll get right on that.

Seatwork:

In this chapter, we talked about how God used the enemy to protect His people. Read Jeremiah 40 for another unusual occurrence of this. Did you find it? Which unexpected person did God use to protect His prophet?

_____

_____

Go deeper with *But in Mount Zion*:
- Read "This Things is From Me."
- Quote: when God's children stray, He goes to extraordinary lengths to win us back. Sometimes, He prunes small, dead, or unproductive branches from the vine. Sometimes, He removes Himself from the vineyard and lets brambles take over. And sometimes, He uses unexpected instruments to accomplish His redemption. In this section, we'll study all three.

Part 4

EDOM'S VIOLENCE REPAID

13

Mic Drop

I will bring thee down, saith the Lord.
Obadiah 4

Edom, God declares throughout Scripture, will have her turn in the principal's office (talk about an extended metaphor). However, in His cups-running-over mercy, He gave them plenty of heads-up and a final chance to get their hearts right. In His perpetual fairness, He warned them of the comeuppance heading their way, and Obadiah was one of the prophets He used to do it.

Fruit Basket Turnover! Time to scramble things up again as we enter a new section of the study:

1. Edom's violence repaid
    a. Arrogance and foolish boasting (2–4)
    b. Wrath prophesied (5–7)
    c. Wrath played out (8–9, 10b, 15–16)

Per our handy-dandy outline, we will now head back to verses 2–9. This is the point where we talk about exactly what's going to happen to Edom because of their hatred toward God's Chosen. They had their fun during Jerusalem's downfall, but they did *not* have the last laugh.

So, what happened, and who pulled the plug on this kingdom?

> Behold, I have made thee small among the heathen: thou art greatly despised. The pride of thine heart hath deceived thee, thou that dwellest in the clefts of the rock, whose habitation is high; that saith in his heart, who shall bring me down to the ground? Though thou exalt thyself as the eagle, and though thou set thy nest among the stars, thence will I bring thee down, saith the Lord. (Obadiah 2–4)

From Nebuchadnezzar's perspective, his army and his captain of the guard, Nebuzaradan, were responsible for Edom's destruction, but God makes it clear in the Book of Obadiah that this punishment comes from Him. In Obadiah's following verses, He gives the reason for it.

"Behold," God begins. "See! Watch!"

This first word tells us right up front that the decree God's about to let loose is not an idle threat. There would be eyewitnesses to the hammer falling. Until that day arrived, God would describe it for them.

Them who? The Edomites for starters. God on his throne spoke directly to the Kingdom of Edom. We'll go ahead and add their name in there to really drive it home. "Behold [Edom], I have made thee small among the heathen."

Let's stop there for a second. Remember how I said that the Jews were Obadiah's intended audience? If that's so, then why is God speaking to the Edomites? Great question. It's one I had, too.

Look at it this way. In this passage, God is allowing Obadiah to witness His decree of judgment against the Edomites. Kind of like the person who signs a marriage license as a witness, confirming the contract is legit. God's warning was legally witnessed, recorded, and disseminated. None will ever be able to refute His mercy.

Even though God is speaking to Edom, He wants His people to hear it, to be reassured God has not forgotten them but will avenge them and restore them to their homeland. The message is also a cautionary tale for anyone considering similar behavior. Finally, God is glorified when His prophecies are fulfilled. And this one *was* fulfilled.

In the first phrase of Obadiah 2, does your translation read in the past tense?

KJV:	I have made thee small
NKJV:	I will make you small
ESV:	I will make you small

If so, understand this is not recounting what has already happened. We can call the past tense that's used here "prophetic past." It's used as a device to convey the sense that the event is *as good as* over and done[1]. That's how certain this prophecy is—already finished. God spoke it. It's done. They just don't know it yet.

To be made small, Edom must have been a kingdom to boast about, right? Actually, historical and archaeological evidence reveal the opposite. Nothing about Edom, apart from their unscalable mountains and their control of valuable trade routes from Southern Arabia, could place her anywhere close to the great powers of her time.

In modern terms, the kingdom can't even be classified as a national "state," since it was made up of loosely centralized nomadic tribes. It wasn't until later in their rule that they became sedentary and established small villages, and most of those were wiped out when the Assyrians took charge[2] (900–600 BC).

Despite its relatively minor existence, Edom was known for its pride, treachery, greed, and violence. Remember what Jeremiah had to say about them? "Thy terribleness hath deceived thee, and the pride of thine heart, O thou that dwellest in the clefts of the rock" (49:16).

Because they held "the height of the hill" and lived among the griffin vultures and imperial eagles, their warriors would have been rough and hardy, surefooted and fearless. The outlaw/banditti type, they would have thrived on guerrilla warfare.[3] They knew every niche and crevice and could squirrel themselves away in a flash. Invading forces didn't have a chance.

Until God. Until He said, "Enough."

He gave them Mount Seir way back when (Gen. 36:8, Deut. 2:22), and everything they had was by His grace. As humans are prone to do, they forgot all about that. Forgot about God altogether.

Over time, they grew proud and brutal in their strength, safe in their "nest among the stars." They boasted, "Who shall bring me down to the ground?" They meant it as a rhetorical question with "no one" as the answer, but the Lord spoke right up in a statement that gives me chills.

"From thence," He says, "I will bring thee down."

Mic. Drop.

Edom's cliffs might have been insurmountable, outside the capabilities of man, but God is no man. (Did anyone else just have a *Lord of the Rings* moment?) His reach is unending, and if He ever felt it necessary, He could pluck the stars from their "nest" and use them to burn the world down.

Compare Edom's prideful attitude to Job's. In his darkest moments, when he could not sense God, he cried out:

> Behold, I go forward, but he is not there; and backward, but I cannot perceive him: On the left hand, where he doth work, but I cannot behold him: he hideth himself on the right hand, that I cannot see him: But he knoweth the way that I take: when he hath tried me, I shall come forth as gold. My foot hath held his steps, his way have I kept, and not declined. And what his soul desireth, even that he doeth. And [Job] said, Naked came I out of my mother's womb, and naked shall I return thither: the Lord gave, and the Lord hath taken

away; blessed be the name of the Lord. (Job 1:21; 23:8–11, 13b)

Even when we can't see God, He's there. His almighty hand can reach us anywhere, whether to embrace, to sustain, or to discipline. And what God gives, He can absolutely take away. Unfortunately, unlike Job, the Edomites never figured that out.

Coming up, we'll learn in precise terms exactly how hard that lesson was for them to learn.

Pop Quiz:

Obadiah's intended audience was:

A.) the eagles nesting on the heights.

B.) the Edomites dwelling next to the nesting eagles on the heights.

C.) the Judeans because of the violent Edomites who dwell next to the nesting eagles on the heights.

14

Hammer Time

How are the things of Esau searched out!
How are his hidden things sought up!
Obadiah 6

In the next five verses, God gets real with His judgment. No more broad threats of "you'll be made small...greatly despised...brought down." The Edomites are told in clear terms how their high-and-mightiness will receive its end. God lists five things that are going to happen to them:

1) They'll be plundered.
2) They'll be driven away when they plead for help from their allies.
3) They'll be betrayed by those they believed to be their friends.
4) Their wise men will be made stupid.
5) Their inhabitants will be cut off and slaughtered.

If you had déjà vu reading that, you're not alone. A peek at Obadiah 15 tells us why it's so familiar. "As thou hast done, it shall be done unto thee: thy reward shall return upon thine own head." In its recent past, Edom did those exact things to another nation (hint: it was Judah). The Judeans had not forgotten, and here, in these five verses, God is saying that He hasn't either. He will revisit Edom's sin upon her.

Wickedness does not go unnoticed or unpunished, especially regarding God's Chosen. And that goes both ways. God diligently guards His children, but He also expects more from them.

Esau was a child of Abraham just like Jacob. He started out as a (presumably) circumcised child of the Covenant, same as his twin, Jacob. At one time, he probably worshipped Yahweh in the same manner as his father and brother, but in the centuries that followed, he and his descendants veered off God's path and created their own gods made of stone.

The hammer didn't fall right away, because "The Lord is longsuffering, and of great mercy, forgiving iniquity and transgression, and by no means clearing the guilty, visiting the iniquity of the fathers upon the children unto the third and fourth generation" (Num. 14:18).

Isaiah 65 gives us an instance of God's longsuffering with Judah reaching its end. In Obadiah, His patience has run out on the Edomites. They took their wickedness one step too far, and now, they're going to suffer the consequences.

I'd imagine certain Edomites got their hands on Obadiah's prophecy. I wonder how they felt after reading his warning. Did they blow it off? Or did they feel like a kid sent to their room to wait for dad to get home?

Remember that feeling, waiting for righteous judgment from your parent? And you knew you totally deserved it, too. You *really* shouldn't have stolen your sister's stamp, then squabbled with her at 120 decibels while claiming it was yours. (Just so we're clear, that stamp *was* mine.)

There might have been a few Edomites who truly trembled, but I believe most of them read these lines and laughed at the absurdness of it all. Could the enemy reach their mountaintop cities? Pfft. Unlikely. Plunder them to bare bones? No way.

Oh, you just wait, Edom. It's coming.

Indeed, two millennia ago, God came and went over Edom, and we can be certain He did exactly as He promised. Which was Thing 1 from "God's list of awful consequences":

1) Plunder them.

Last month, while my family was enjoying our endless salad and breadsticks at Olive Garden, some devious soul was breaking into our car in broad daylight. They took a messenger bag from the backseat. Apart from my daughter's sketch pad, they scored a whopping ten bucks. If they'd been braver, they might have checked the glove compartment and been a little happier with their spoils. But that's a thief's typical behavior, isn't it? Dash in. Snatch and grab. Skedaddle.

Contrast that with what's described in Obadiah. Their dwellings will be "searched out," and their most valuable possessions will be sought after. This is no middle-of-the-night sneaky Grinch event. No tiptoeing about while the Whos are sleeping.

> If thieves came to thee, if robbers by night, (how art thou cut off!) would they not have stolen till they had enough? if the grape-gatherers came to thee, would they not leave some grapes? How are the things of Esau searched out! how are his hidden things sought up!
> (Obadiah 5-6)

This is a thorough pillaging. Furniture overturned. Mattresses gutted. Drywall busted in. Coffee can dumped. They want Granny's jewelry, and they're not going to stop until they find it.

The Edomites would be "cut off," meaning utterly destroyed. Nothing would be left. Not even their lineage. (More on this "utter destruction" in the next chapter.)

One way they were plundered hit them in the heart of their arrogance—their vineyards. At this reference to grapes in relation to Edom, my nerdy heart claps its tiny nerdy hands. In recent decades, archaeology has proven the kingdom of Edom was known for its vineyards (score another point for biblical accuracy!). And God knew a strike to that aspect of their pride would be a particularly humbling blow.

But what exactly is meant by "grape gatherers"? There are two possible interpretations. It could be referring to legit gleaners or to raiders. According to Hebraic law (Lev. 19:9–10), gleaners, meaning the poor and those traveling through, were allowed to take a small portion of every harvest. The description of "grape gatherers" has a mild, mundane connotation, and it's odd to use a practice approved by the Law as a comparison for the atrocities that would come from God's judgment.

That's probably why Bible scholars present a second possible meaning—those who raid vineyards outside the law. Grape pirates, so to speak. Typically, same as our satchel thief, this type of thief would have kept their business to bagging what they could and hightailing it before the dogs woke up.

Which of these two options are you feeling? Don't stress about it too much because either interpretation yields the same answer to the rhetorical questions in verse 5:

Q. Would they not have stolen till they had enough?
A. Yep, thieves usually steal only until they have their arms full. So they don't trip during their getaway.
Q. If grape gatherers had come to you, would they not leave some grapes?
A. That's right. Grape gathers, legal or otherwise, rarely strip a vine bare.

The Edomite invaders didn't have to worry about tripping because they weren't in a hurry.

They had all the time in the world to turn the kingdom upside down, which is the implied point of these verse's 5 lines—what normally happens will not happen this time.

Also, less obvious in this section is what is *not* said. Whenever God punished Israel and Judah for their wickedness, He always provided a way back to Him and promised to leave a remnant.

Here's a tiny sample of God working to ensure there's a fragment left in the wake of destruction:

> **Noah and the flood**: And every living substance was destroyed which was upon the face of the ground, both man, and cattle, and the creeping things, and the fowl of the heaven; and they were destroyed from the earth: and Noah only remained alive, and they that were with him in the ark. (Gen. 7:23)

> **Joseph and the famine**: And God sent me before you to preserve you a posterity in the earth, and to save your lives by a great deliverance. (Gen. 45:7)

> **Elijah escapes Jezebel**: Yet I have left me seven thousand in Israel, all the knees which have not bowed unto Baal, and every mouth which hath not kissed him. (1 Kings 19:18)

> **Israel taken captive by Assyria**: Therefore the Lord was very angry with Israel, and removed them out of his sight: there was none left but the tribe of Judah only. (2 Kings 17:18)

God promises to leave a remnant: Yet will I leave a remnant, that ye may have some that shall escape the sword among the nations, when ye shall be scattered through the countries. (Ezek. 6:8)

God's punishment is not full destruction: Fear thou not, O Jacob my servant, saith the Lord: for I am with thee; for I will make a full end of all the nations whither I have driven thee: but I will not make a full end of thee, but correct thee in measure; yet will I not leave thee wholly unpunished. (Jer. 46:28)

The remnant returns to Israel: The remnant shall return, even the remnant of Jacob, unto the mighty God. (Isa. 10:21)

In the first four, we see God in action. In the last three, we hear God's vow before the event to "leave a remnant" when the Assyrians and Babylonians invade and take the covenant people captive (a vow that is fulfilled in Nehemiah).

God grants Edom no such promise. They were to be gutted. Stripped. Reduced to nothing.

That's clear. The question remains, how? Edom was impenetrable.

Apart from the fact that God isn't hindered by land or sea, height or depth, treachery was involved in Edom's summary downfall. That brings us to Thing 2 and Thing 3:

2) They'll be driven away when they plea for help from their allies.

3) They'll be betrayed by those they believed to be their friends.

We find the above two prophecies in Obadiah seven.

> All the men of thy confederacy have brought thee even to the border: the men that were at peace with thee have deceived thee, and prevailed against thee; they that eat thy bread have laid a wound under thee: there is none understanding in him.
> (Obadiah 7)

The phrase "men of your confederacy" is circumlocution for the much simpler term "allies." (You probably already figured that out—I just wanted to use *circumlocution*. All the logophiles in the room, raise your hands.) The literal translation of that phrase is "men of your covenant." These are men with whom the Edomites had formed official bonds, probably political. It implies the parties are on an equal plane. Each has something to offer the other.

"Men at peace with you," on the other hand, suggests there had been war or the threat of war between the two entities. The image it invokes is that of a greater kingdom choosing peace with the weaker one instead of monkey stomping them into submission.

Because of the variations in those two phrases, this verse seems to be talking about two separate groups and possibly separate incidences.

After digging through my sources of historical record, I couldn't find any specific mention of Edomite allies, but according to Obadiah 7, they had at least one. Kingdoms typically did. It was just smart politics. You watch my back. I'll watch yours.

Which kingdom, then, could this verse mean? Review the map of Edom on page 45, taking note of the nations bordering Edom. The closest was Moab with the Nabatu and Arabian tribes taking up Edom's east and west flanks. We can be certain the verse doesn't mean Judah because, at this point, they'd probably already been sacked and reduced to rubble.

Whoever the allies were, Edomite officials entered their land for a meeting or a request, only to be repelled. Something went terribly awry. Maybe the Edomites proposed rebellion against their overlords, the Babylonians, and the other party wasn't having it. Or maybe they filched a few invaluable Anulax batteries and incited an ~~intergalactic~~ international incident.

My personal favorite? They went asking for assistance or refuge because they were *already under attack*. The neighboring kingdom knew better than to get on Babylon's bad side, so they promptly showed them the door, leaving a boot print on their backsides, Nabonidus style.

Why is this my favorite? Because this theory directly parallels their treatment of Judah when she was under attack and her people were scattering like ants looking for hidey-holes. Shall we sneak another peek at Obadiah 15? We shall. "As you have done, it shall be done to you; Your reprisal shall return upon your own head." More on this soon, promise.

147

So, that's the allies covered. What about the "men that were at peace with you" phrase? One guess who that could be. Ding, ding, ding! Babylonia.

When I search the anthropology database of my university's library, I get dozens of hits for Edom. I have yet to find a journal that debates the decade of Edom's demise (550s BC). In fact, one archaeologist narrows it down to a specific year. Dr. Crowell references a relief discovered on a sandstone cliffside in 1994. He uses it to land the timeline needle on 551 BC. He even reconstructs a believable story of how it happened.

The story goes like this.

During Babylon's campaign against Judah, Edom did not come to their aid, despite being treaty partners. After, they hunted down refugees and handed them over to the enemy, thus avoiding General Nebuzaradan's wrath.

After the Babylonian army left the region, the area opened wide for new settlers. To give a little perspective, before Judah got on Babylon's bad side, Jerusalem's population had been approximately 6,000. By the time Nebuzaradan was finished, a total of 4,600 had been taken into captivity. "How doth the city sit solitary, that was full of people!" Jeremiah cries in Lamentations 1:1. Not everyone, however, was taken.

This is where the remnant comes in. "But the captain of the guard [Nebuzaradan] left of the poor of the land to be vinedressers and husbandmen" (2 Kings 25:12). These few were the ones blessed with watching their homes and land being overrun by their greedy neighbors.

Confetti raining down, the Edomites leaped to fill the gap the Judeans had left behind by moving into the Arabah. There's also indication in Obadiah that the Edomites moved into Jerusalem. Going so far as to live in the Jews' homes, they "laid hands on their substance" (Obad. 13). Really, guys? You should know better.

For thirty years, they got away with it, prospering as they never had before. The elite, especially, benefited by gaining a firm grasp on the commerce and trade routes to Arabia. As their pockets grew, so did their heads. It was this greed and pride that ultimately led to their end.

The more you have, the bigger the target you become. Since Judah's humiliation, Edom had acquired a lot of land, and the average citizen's wealth increased across the board. What they did not increase was their military might.

They remained the weak collection of tribes they'd always been and, ultimately, didn't have the strength to hold onto their stolen goods. No fool, Babylonian King Nabonidus was fully aware of the unprotected wealth Edom was sitting on. *Cue Scrooge McDuck rubbing his hands in gleeful anticipation.

At the time, Edom still consisted mostly of small, unfortified villages that labored mainly in agriculture. Three strong-ish cities existed, but only one was walled and defendable against a force as imposing as Babylon.

Edom had built that fortified city high on a lateral ridge extending out from a mountain. Deep ravines dropped away on three sides. Today, the ruins are called (can you guess??) Busayra (Bozrah in Hebrew). Do you see where this is going? Yeah, me too, and it's giving me another bout of amaze-bumps.

This moment deserves another jam on that Pause button so we can reread Jeremiah 49:13. "For I have sworn by myself, saith the Lord, that Bozrah shall become a desolation, a reproach, a waste, and a curse; and all the cities thereof shall be perpetual wastes." Then there's Amos's words against it. "But I will send a fire upon Teman, which shall devour the palaces of Bozrah" (Amos 1:12).

Clearly, Bozrah was predicted to crumble and burn, but it wasn't "a waste" at the time of Obadiah's writing. So, what happened? What wasted it? Who?

For decades, that question has been much discussed and debated among historians and archaeologists, but the answer is finally starting to firm up. Which I can't wait to tell you about in chapter 16.

For now, it's enough to know that Edom was betrayed by someone who'd sworn peace with

> The men that were at peace with thee have deceived thee, and prevailed against thee; they that eat thy bread have laid a wound under thee.
> (Obadiah 7b)

them. Someone who had sat down with them and shared a meal.

In ancient days, mealtimes were almost sacred. Sharing food was a symbol of goodwill. When a person sits down to eat, they're assuming a vulnerable position. They're putting aside their weapons and filling their hands with food. Hard to defend oneself using figs and flatbread.

In many Eastern cultures—both then and now—when enemies are invited to eat, they are not enemies for the duration of the meal. They can each rest assured they are safe. One does not violate the time-honored custom of hospitality. Unless, of course, you're one of these treacherous yahoos.

There's archaeological evidence describing how Edomite diplomats visited Babylonia's capital over the years to learn, pay tribute, and report to the king. Because roads go both ways, there's a high likelihood Babylonian officials traveled to Edom as well. Once in Edom, their hosts would have received them with all courtesy and offered them refreshments.

It's possible Babylon got wind of Edomite rebellion, sent their diplomats and accompanying retinue under the guise of a peaceful conference, and launched a surprise attack. Or could be Edom went down with all the rest in a broad militaristic sweep. Just another crushed bug in King Nabonidus's campaign of theft and subjugation.

Did the attack happen *while* they were eating? Who knows. But these "men at peace" with them had at some point shared a meal, sealing their friendship.

Keep in mind that these are theories reconstructed from the few details the Bible provides combined with scholarly opinion derived from scraps of Babylonian imperial records (plus a little Gardner imagination, which goes to town in *A Hope Fulfilled*). It's fun to try piecing it together, but we won't call it Holy Spirit inspired.

In whatever way the destruction happened, the Edomites did *not* see it coming. That we do know for sure. Despite a prophecy detailing their doom (which they may or may not have received), they were completely blindsided. As we'll see in Obadiah verse 8, they were stunned stupid.

Pop Quiz:
Name two biblical characters in the line of David who were betrayed by someone who had eaten with them.

_____

_____

_____

15

Eye for an Eye

...as thou hast done, it shall be done unto thee.
Obadiah 15

Obadiah's verse 8 reminds us that this prophecy is no vague event sometime in the future. The destruction would happen on a particular day. "In that day," God declares. He uses that phrase often in Scripture, and it's almost always in reference to prophecy, meaning that at a specific point in time, He will inject His almighty Self into human affairs with either judgment or salvation.

> Shall I not in that day, saith the Lord, even destroy the wise men out of Edom, and understanding out of the mount of Esau? And thy mighty men, O Teman, shall be dismayed, to the end that every one of the mount of Esau may be cut off by slaughter.
> (Obadiah 8–9)

In this instance, He would muddle the Edomites' brains. Have you ever been so shocked and terrified, you lost the ability to think?

My husband and I are beekeepers. Last month, we visited our hives at night to carry out a small task that can't be done during the day while the girls are all out on the job. We couldn't use a light because then the bees would take flight and not be able to find their way home once the lights went off. So, pitch-black bee handling it was.

On a relevant side note, I was aware there was a bee-sized hole in the veil of my suit—and that bees often target the eyes. With that at the forefront of my mind, I began this very small task, which happened to set them off in a very large way.

They came pouring out of the entrance like spiders from the drain in *Arachnophobia*, tiny black monsters, each with the ability to put out an eye. Or so my "dismayed" brain was telling me when I realized one of them was crawling inside my veil.

In the same instant, an especially sneaky bee got through a gap in my glove and stung me on the wrist. After that, all I remember is screaming and running toward the truck while being unable to unzip my veil to get *out*.

My husband had a different (admittedly more amusing) perspective. By his account, I was actually running in circles and slamming into low-hanging cedar branches. Again and again.

And turns out, the bee was never on the inside of the veil. By the time my husband chased me down and rescued me (from myself), she'd crawled to the back of the hood. Make no mistake, she was looking for my eyes, but she wasn't anywhere close.

Suffice it to say, that wasn't my shiniest moment. I lost my mind, quite literally, and can't remember half of what I did. My security behind the veil had been ripped away. The bee had breached my walls. To my stunned, stupid dismay, the enemy was *within*.

In the case of the Edomites, the Babylonians really had breached their ramparts and were within their walls. The enemy was suddenly in their homes, in their vineyards, in every place they never should have been. Their cliff-top sanctuary was supposed to be unreachable, undefeatable.

But God.

What was it He said in verse 3? "I will bring thee down." That's it. On His order, there the enemy was, right at their very steep doorstep.

The impossibility of it all was too much for them to grasp. Their understanding of reality had been upended, and in their shock and panic, the Edomite warriors' wisdom and training became consternation and dismay. It was so bad the entire kingdom was "cut off by slaughter" (Obad. 9; Jer. 49:7).

Tragically, the "cutting off" didn't end with Babylon's invasion. God goes a step further in Obadiah 10 by declaring Edom would be "cut off *forever*." Which brings us to...

Another round of everyone's favorite game. Fruit Basket Turnover. And...go! I know you're excited, ladies, but no shoving. Once everyone has found a seat, you should find yourself at Obadiah 15.

> For the day of the Lord is near upon all the heathen: as thou hast done, it shall be done unto thee: thy reward shall return upon thine own head.
> (Obadiah 15)

Does the phrase "the day of the Lord" sound like an echo to you? If so, head back up to verse 8 and find its mirror phrase, "in that day."

With these words, Obadiah begins the book's final act. It's here we have a twist, a shift in tone, and a segue into the final portion of the book. God expands the prophecy to "all the heathen," meaning every nation.

The "day" mentioned here—the judgment of nations—begins with Edom. In Obadiah, Edom has the questionable honor of being the example nation. Judah serves as a model of God's care and discipline of His children, while Edom stands at the opposite end of the spectrum, serving as a warning for those who reject Him.

There's no other nation in the Bible who, while given complete knowledge of and access to Yahweh at its outset, choses to turn its back and walk away. It's true Judah and Israel both did the same over the course of their history, but they always retained some modicum of truth. No matter their Temple practices (or lack of) or the spiritual state of their reigning king, there was always a light. A prophet, a priest, a praying mother.

In contrast, Edom walked away and never looked back. There is zero evidence—either in the Bible or archaeological record—of Yahweh in their midst.

Only Hagar's Ishmael comes close to this my-way, fork-in-the-road backstory, but where he was rejected by Sarah and sent away by Abraham, he was blessed by God for it (Genesis 21). Edom is unique for having started out sheltered by the covenant yet *choosing* to walk out from under it to do her own thing. Because of that, because of "what thou has done," "the day of the Lord is near." According Obadiah's perspective, they were the opening act of God's wrath upon the nations.

At the time of the book's writing, Judah is in the throes of her own "day of the Lord," but the discipline she receives isn't quite the same as what's heading Edom's way. To continue the school/principal analogy, we can say Judah was suspended for bad behavior, while Edom was expelled. Then kicked out of town. Then trampled and scattered and wiped off the map. Forever.

God's discipline of Judah was harsh, but it had an end. As always, there was a remnant left behind, and seventy years later, His children returned to rebuild the Temple and their nation (see Ezra, Nehemiah, and Jeremiah 29:10).

Edom, on the other hand, was told she would be wiped from history, from existence. No take backs.

Obadiah says it four times:

1. "thou shalt be cut off for ever" (10)
2. "[Edom] shall be as though they had not been" (16)
3. "the house of Esau [shall be] stubble" (18)
4. "there shall not be any remaining of the house of Esau" (18)

And as we've seen, our guy Obadiah isn't the only one saying it. Edom's destruction is a popular theme in the Old Testament.

Ezekiel is all about the gavel banging. Here's one of his. These verses do such a beautiful job of summing it all up.

> Thus saith the Lord God; Because that Edom hath dealt against the house of Judah by taking vengeance, and hath greatly offended, and revenged himself upon them; Therefore thus saith the Lord God; I will also stretch out mine hand upon Edom, and will cut off man and beast from it; and I will make it desolate from Teman; and they of Dedan shall fall by the sword. (Ezek. 25:12)

That's not all he has to say about Edom. His chapters have so much content, I'm going to direct you there for personal reading and study. The passages are Ezekiel 32:29, 36:5, and all of 35. Don't play hooky on these, girlie. You'll miss out! But because of similarity to Obadiah and Joel's messages, there are several verses of that bunch I can't leave unreferenced here.

Because thou hast had a perpetual hatred, and hast shed the blood of the children of Israel by the force of the sword in the time of their calamity, in the time that their iniquity had an end: Therefore, as I live, saith the Lord God, I will prepare thee unto blood, and blood shall pursue thee: sith thou hast not hated blood, even blood shall pursue thee.

Therefore, as I live, saith the Lord God, *I will even do according to* thine anger, and according to thine envy which thou hast used out of thy hatred against them; and I will make myself known among them, when I have judged thee.

Thus saith the Lord God; When the whole earth rejoiceth, I will make thee desolate. As *thou didst rejoice at* the inheritance of the house of Israel, because it was desolate, *so will I do unto thee*: thou shalt be desolate, O mount Seir, and all Idumea, even all of it: and they shall know that I am the Lord. (Ezek. 35:5–6, 11, 14–15, italics mine)

Compare that passage to Obadiah 15–16. In both places, God is pulling out the old eye-for-an-eye law. It was instituted in Exodus 21 and continued in use until Jesus brought in a new order of mercy and grace—at least as far as Christ-followers are concerned (Matt. 3:38–39).

By applying this time-honored method of righting wrongs, God is once again reminding all parties that Edom is both a brother and a neighbor. We've already covered the other reminders in verses 10 and 12, but we can add the command God gave to Israel back in

Deuteronomy: "You shall not abhor an Edomite, for he is your brother" (27:13).

To the end, God considers them family. Distant cousins, sure, but He never gave up on Esau or his descendants. They were, after all, children of Abraham and Isaac and, if they'd made better choices, they could have benefited externally from the Covenant blessing. Instead, they followed their father's example. They rejected the Blessing, created their own god, lived in perpetual bitterness and envy, continually searched out opportunities to cause trouble, and ultimately, shot their brother in the back.

There's one last portion of Scripture I want to cover that really drives home Edom's offenses, listing them out with other nations who did the Hebrews wrong. For full effect, Joel 3 is worth a visit to your Bible, but here it is in brief, laid out in a pattern like the one Obadiah uses but backwards.

Offenses ⟹ Consequences.

The guilty nations...

- scattered God's people "among the nations" (3:2)
- divided up His land (3:3)
- cast lots for His people (3:3)
- gave a boy as payment for a harlot and a girl for wine (3:3)
- took His silver and gold (from the Temple) and used them in their own temples (3:5)
- sold the people of Judah (3:6)

160

- removed them far from their borders (3:6)

In response God will...

- bring again the captivity of Judah and Jerusalem (3:1)
- gather all nations...into the valley of Jehoshaphat (3:2)
- sit and judge those nations (3:2, 12)
- return retaliation upon their heads (3:4, 7)
- sell their descendants into the hand of the people of Judah (3:8)
- dim the sun, moon, and stars (3:15)
- roar from Zion and utter His voice from Jerusalem (3:16)
- shake the heavens and earth (3:16)
- shelter His people (3:16)
- prevent further trespass (3:17)
- bless His people (3:18, 20–21)
- make Egypt a desolation (3:19)
- make Edom a desolate wilderness (3:19)

Bullet points are The Best. I'm a true believer in them. They make such a neat summary. Which is perfect because I don't want to linger in Joel. Not when we have one final question on this section of Obadiah. What's with all the drinking in verse 16?? Here's that verse again.

> For as ye have drunk upon my holy mountain, so
> shall all the heathen drink continually, yea, they
> shall drink, and they shall swallow down, and they
> shall be as though they had not been.
> (Obadiah 16)

Got any initial thoughts? How about this to get you started—what's the first image that "drinking" conjures?

For me, it's my favorite 34-oz. stainless-steel cooler with green rubber straw (seltzer, please). And because brains are weird, the second image that comes to me is that of a painting I visited with my senior class many moons ago on a fieldtrip to the Museo del Prado in Madrid.

I say "odd" because the mild celebration happening in *The Triumph of Bacchus* by Diego Velazquez is nothing like the revelry that took place around the burning of the Temple. Juan de la Corta's *The Burning of Jerusalem by Nebuchadnezzar's Army* comes much closer to the image we're after, except it depicts only terror. The party that took place on "My holy mountain" (the Temple Mount) is quite absent from the scene, but we can be sure it was there.

Just as the Edomites drank in celebration over Judah's destruction, so others will raise a toast when Edom goes down (more of that eye-for-an-eye, eh?). Edom had her day. Now, it's God's turn.

The other nations will drink over Edom's demise, drink some more for emphasis, then swallow, then Edom will "be as though they had not been." This is an echo of Joel 3 where God declares He will exact justice on all those who, over the centuries, despised and wounded His children.

In Scripture, drinking is a common metaphor for judgment and shame. Habakkuk 2:15–16 is a great example, as are Jeremiah 25:17–18 and 28–29. And remember Jeremiah 49 from chapter 13 (pp. 114–6), the passage that parallels Obadiah so closely. Two of its verses tell a similar tale, but they also suggest that Judah had already had to "drink of the cup" of judgment. Eye, meet eye.

> For thus saith the Lord; Behold, they whose judgment was not to drink of the cup have assuredly drunken; and art thou he that shall altogether go unpunished? thou shalt not go unpunished, but thou shalt surely drink of it. For I have sworn by myself, saith the Lord, that Bozrah shall become a desolation, a reproach, a waste, and a curse; and all the cities thereof shall be perpetual wastes. (Jer. 49:12–13)

Despite all this, I believe God would have welcomed Edom back right up until the very end. Through the example of Nineveh in the book of Jonah and through the prophet Jeremiah, God tells us He will welcome any pagan nation that will surrender to Him. Speaking of Babylon, He declared, "And it shall come to pass, if they will diligently learn the ways of my people, to swear by my name, The Lord liveth...then shall they be built in the midst of my people" (Jer. 12:16).

If Edom had sworn "the Lord lives!" would He have taken them in? Absolutely. Would they have been spared punishment? Doubtful. Israel and Judah both suffered the consequences of their rebellion. Edom was destined for the same, but maybe, just maybe, if they'd repented, they wouldn't have been annihilated.

Alas, they did not repent, and as the Lord says in the following verse, "But if they will not obey, I will utterly pluck up and destroy that nation" (Jer. 12:17). As a consequence, Edom was given the Full Pagan Treatment and lumped together with the rest of the foreign nations who acted out against Israel. They were promised no remnant. They were given no hope of restoration.

Their bonus punishment was that their destruction was absolute and final. God wrote The End across their page of history and smeared them out so thoroughly that, today, we're hazy on the details.

In the next chapter, we'll go into what we *do* know about Edom's last gasping breaths.

Pop Quiz:

The name Teman came up again in this chapter. Which "friend" in the Bible hailed from Teman? Do you think God might be making an ironic allusion to the stunned stupid Edomites?

_____

_____

_____

16

Nabonidus Was Here

The men that were at peace with thee have deceived thee.
Obadiah 7a

During the years 553–550 BC, King Nabonidus of Babylon took his army on a campaign of destruction. History is crystal clear on this. Four ancient Babylonian texts have been discovered that mention this expedition, but they're only partial readings, forcing scholars to read between the few words that time has not managed to erase.

However, thanks to those texts, archaeologists know that 1) Nabonidus's aim during his campaign was to reach the desert oasis of Tayma in Arabia, and 2) on the way, his army traversed land characterized as being a "terrain of hardship," and having "difficult routes" and "(places) where passage is prevented and no feet go."[1]

Those descriptions appear shortly before the text segues into talk of defeating King Dadanu in North Arabia. As far as timeline and geography go, that lines Edom up on the path Nabonidus took. As the map shows, Edom would have been the last kingdom his legions crossed before entering Arabia.

For many years, that was all archaeologists had as far as clues into Edom's destruction, but it was enough to prompt assumptions that Nabonidus wiped out Edom along the way. Not a terrible theory. Then, in 1994, the as-Sila relief of Nabonidus was discovered on a sandstone cliffside, and scholars put their thinking caps back on.

As-Sila was a mountaintop settlement so precariously perched that pictures of it are enough to make you dizzy. It was there, on the side of that mountain, at an almost-impossible-to-reach location, Nabonidus had a relief of himself etched into stone.

Due to copyright, I haven't included an image of the actual etching, but the Harran Stela at the British Museum has one that's a near match (a Google search of "as-Sila relief of Nabonidus" will get you to the actual image). They both depict Nabonidus in his conical (kingly) hat, standing in profile with his right hand raised, holding a staff, and praying to three divine symbols: the moon, the sun, and Venus.

The as-Sila inscription, archaeologists speculate, was probably engraved to commemorate Edom's complete subjugation on

Nabonidus's route to Tayma. At the very least, it was placed there to mark his passing through, whether violent or peaceful—just like a gangster tagging an overpass to say "8-ball was here." Except Nabonidus's lackeys skipped the spray paint and went straight to the chisel—300 feet above the ground. He even wrote his version of "Nabonidus was here" beside the figure.

Basalt Stela of Nabonidus[2]
Attribution: British Museum

This week, my National Parks Geography professor (best course ever) has me at a cemetery studying tombstones and weathering. My town's little graveyard goes back to the 1880s. That's not even 150 years ago, yet I've been squinting hard to read dates and names etched into marble and granite. How archaeologists can read etchings on *sandstone* from two millennia ago blows my mind. But, indeed, their instruments and trained eyes have picked up traces of cuneiform that have provided substantial clues into what went on that year in Edom.

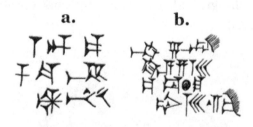

(Attribution: Babylonian Cuneiform[3])

The smart people of the world have determined that the above scratchings (cuneiform) read as follows:

a. I am Nabû-na'id, king of Babylon
[. . .] Samas the [great] lord . . .
[. . .] Sîn [. . .]

b. Year 5 [. . .
the troop]s [. . .
. . .] the gate of [. . .
. . .] the men [. . .

"Nabunai'd" is an alternate, less common, spelling of Nabonidus, and "year 5" indicates the year of his reign. "Samas" and "Sîn" are names of two of the deities in the relief (sun and moon respectively).

In other words, we can put together that at some point in the fifth year of his reign (551 BC), Nabonidus was tagging a mountain in Edom.[4] Why? A question for the ages.

We know for a fact that he was on campaign to Tayma, which was a road of violence, conquering, and accruing wealth. No historical evidence definitively connects him with an attack on any Edomite city, but when the dots are lined up, his purpose there starts smelling suspiciously like conquer-slaughter-destroy-take (Obad. 5–9).

One last point: the settlement of as-Sila was located directly on a critical trade route (King's Highway). Why wouldn't a power-hungry king want it for himself? Let's say he did destroy Edom. King Nabonidus is guilty as charged. The next question becomes, did he do it?

It couldn't have been an easy defeat, even for a trained army (see this chapter's seatwork for pictures). There's no reason, he couldn't have entered Edom under their typical flag of peace then turned on them.

Greed is a powerful motivator, and we can assume Nabonidus *really* wanted their copper resources as well as control of the mountain passes. The best way into those fortress-type mountains would have been to be invited. "Why fight your way in if you can walk through the gate?" Tikvah asks in *A Hope Fulfilled*.[5]

In whatever way it occurred, according to Obadiah, deception was at play, and it involved an entity Edom had once welcomed as guests at their dinner.

That concludes Edom's horrific downfall. Coming up, the verses everyone has been waiting for. The grand finale. Judah's ultimate deliverance and Jesus's triumphal reign. Doesn't get much better than this, y'all.

But first, real quick, check out the pics of as-Sila's ruins by following the links in the seatwork below.

Seatwork:

Visit the American Society of Overseas Research for some crazy-interesting pictures of ancient Edom's topography, the ruins of as-Sila (hold on to your stomach), and the location of the relief: https://www.asor.org/anetoday/2019/03/New-Discoveries-at-Sela/

The Biblical Archaeological Society gives a close-up of the relief: www.biblicalarchaeology.org/daily/the-nabonidus-inscription-at-sela/

Go deeper with *But in Mount Zion*:
- Read "Behold Their Threatenings."
- Quote: In this segment, we'll be covering the topic of threats. Empty threats. Threats with a bite. Threats that frustrate the Enemy. Threats that compel us to fall to our knees before God and plead, "Behold their threatenings!"

Part 5

JUDAH'S ULTIMATE VICTORY

17

Three Blessings

But upon mount Zion shall be deliverance.
Obadiah 17

We have arrived! Announcing the last portion of our study of Obadiah.

2. Judah's ultimate victory
    a. Three blessings (17–18)
    b. Three promises (17–18)
    c. Jesus Messiah will reign (19–21)

Quite frankly, I've dreaded tackling these last five verses, especially 19–21 because I had so many questions. Still do. Always will. My brain never stops with the questions! These verses in Obadiah, from 17 to the end, have been studied and debated for centuries, and scholars can't seem to agree on their exact meaning. I'm right there with them.

Not a resounding endorsement of what's supposed to be a climactic ending to a Bible study, eh? I know, I know. But full transparency has always been my motto, so here I am, just another girl struggling to understand the Lord's message to His people. But as always, in His goodness and grace, He's guided me to a basic understanding that I've grown excited about. It starts with one word.

"But."

A small word. A most beautiful word. Here, it announces a shift from promises of enemy annihilation to promises of Israel's deliverance.

Verse 17 houses three blessings that almost slip past the modern Christian but would have brought tears to the eyes of the captive Jews. I'd like you to pause here and take a minute to find and underline those blessings, to think of all they contain, and to consider what they might mean.

> But upon mount Zion shall be deliverance, and there shall be holiness; and the house of Jacob shall possess their possessions.
> (Obadiah 17)

How about another handy-dandy numbered list?

Three blessings for the Jews:

1. Deliverance on Mount Zion
2. Holiness
3. Possession of possessions

Such a pretty collection of promises. We'll pick them apart, but first, more underlining. This time, three promises.

> And the house of Jacob shall be a fire, and the house of Joseph a flame, and the house of Esau for stubble, and they shall kindle in them, and devour them; and there shall not be any remaining of the house of Esau; for the Lord hath spoken it.
> (Obadiah 18)

Find them? Here they are, three promises for the captive Jews:

1. Israel will become a fire/flame
2. Edom will become stubble/consumed
3. Esau's line will be wiped out

These aren't as pretty. I mean, they involve blood and death and a big The End to the offspring of a child of God gone astray. In our humanity, we are tempted to rejoice at the destruction of the wicked, but let's curb that urge.

It's easy to forget these were real people. Real, confused, misguided, deceived, *lost* people. As we move forward, we must be careful to keep that at the front of our minds.

Getting back on track, do you think these two verses are pointing to A) Babylonia's destruction of Edom or to B) a future day, maybe one we have yet to witness? Could they mean *both*? I say option C. We'll spend the next three chapters chatting about how that's possible and discussing each option in its turn.

A) Three Blessings (near fulfillment)

Deliverance, holiness, possession: three blessings that have both a pre- and a post-Messiah fulfillment. In this section, we'll cover the pre-Messiah stuff.

Two hundred years before Obadiah and 500-ish before Nehemiah's reconstructed Temple, God spoke through Amos, the prophet, saying,

> In that day will I raise up the tabernacle of David that is fallen, and close up the breaches thereof; and I will raise up his ruins, and I will build it as in the days of old: That they may possess the remnant of Edom, and of all the heathen, which are called by my name, saith the Lord that doeth this. (Amos 9:11–12)

Here, God proclaimed that He would rebuild the Temple for more than the displaced Jews. With every stone mortared back into place, the Edomites and "all the heathen" were on God's mind.

These verses point to two periods—the day Cyrus issued an edict that allowed the Jews to return from captivity to rebuild, and a day far beyond that when gentiles came into the Church. Here, Edom is once again being used as a representative of all those outside the fold of His Chosen who are "called by [His] name," a.k.a. Believers.

Are you, like me, suddenly seeing yourself as part of this picture? I've never stepped foot on the Temple Mount, never even been to Jerusalem, but

I feel my soul there covered in the Blood of sacrifice. I hear my name on God's lips as He calls me by His name. Sweetest sound in the world, sister. It'll be even sweeter in person. And these days, as we watch the world disintegrate around us, that moment can't come fast enough.

Meanwhile, we'll dig into the Word, know Him better, and cling to His promises for *us*. Oh yeah, and we got to finish out these last verses of Obadiah.

In recent chapters, we've spent a lot of time in the decades beyond Obadiah's day, so it doesn't hurt to remind ourselves here that at the time he wrote his book, the Jews were still in bondage in Babylonia. All they had to cling to was the promise of one day returning to Judah to rebuild.

Other prophets of the age, such as Jeremiah, gave them the hope that their current captors and tormentors would eventually be destroyed (Jer. 51), but Obadiah reminds them that justice would be exacted against Edom, too. All the way back in Numbers, Balaam had prophesied that Edom would "be a possession" (Num. 24:18–19). Obadiah refreshes that promise here and gives it a shiny new gleam.* God is faithful, Obadiah assures the captives. He has not forgotten His word. He will deliver.

"Deliverance" in verse 17 suggests liberation from destruction or bondage. And where will it happen? On Mount Zion.

The Jews would have been familiar with this reference since salvation is often said to come out of the Temple Mount. "The Lord hear thee in the day of trouble," King David says in Psalm 20. "The name of the God of Jacob defend thee; Send thee help from the sanctuary, and strengthen thee out of Zion." And later, in what might be considered a prophetic song, he writes, "Oh that the salvation of Israel were come out of Zion! When God bringeth back the captivity of his people, Jacob shall rejoice, and Israel shall be glad" (Ps. 3:6). They were glad, Your Majesty.

They were especially so when the Temple was rebuilt, sacrifices were reinstated, and holiness was restored. As God promised, the remnant returned and the flame of the "dead" house of Jacob was rekindled. It roared into a fire once again.

In holy justice, the Jews once again "possessed their possessions." The day this oracle was written, the Edomites occupied land sworn to the house of Jacob by Yahweh Himself. They were living high on the hog, rolling in the dough, swimming in gold coins á la Scrooge McDuck. All at the expense of the miserable, captive Jews. The blessing of reclaiming their possessions had to have wrenched a smile up the cheeks of even the most despondent Jewish slave.

Because we have two chapters to go on these verses, let's sum up what we've covered so far so we stay on track. Verse 17 lists three blessings—deliverance, holiness, possession—that are easy to see as already fulfilled. The Jews returned from captivity, rebuilt the Temple (where holy ritual was reinstated), and repossessed lands taken by the Edomites.

177

Simple. Indisputable.

Moving on, we'll examine those three promises you picked out of verse 18 and talk about how they've been fulfilled too. We'll go into a historical event that casts the verse's "devouring" in a light you never would have seen coming.

Seatwork:

Write out these three hope-inspiring verses on deliverance and underline any similarities between them.

Joel 2:32

_____
_____
_____
_____

Isaiah 37:31–32

_____
_____
_____
_____
_____

Obadiah 21

_____
_____
_____
_____
_____

*Shinier than they could even imagine! More on this coming up...

18

Three Promises

There shall not be any remaining of the house of Esau;
for the Lord hath spoken it.
Obadiah 18b

You're back! So glad I haven't lost you to all this deep, heady content. If you're going a little cross-eyed, just think of me in a bee suit, screaming, running in circles in the dark, and slamming into trees.

Attribution: Dumb hooman[1]

There, that did it. Happy to bee of assistance. Now, back to work.

Brief recap. Obadiah 18 focuses on three promises God gives the Jews. Israel will become a fire/flame. Edom will become stubble/consumed. Esau's line will be wiped out.

First, we'll go over how these have already been fulfilled, then we'll rope in those three blessings from the last chapter and look at them all through Future Glasses in part C.

B) Three Promises (near fulfillment)

We've already established that Edom was still around during the Jews' exile in Babylon. Jeremiah and Ezekiel confirm that for us. There's also archaeological evidence in excavations at Ezion-gebet that points to Edom's existence in the mid-500s.

But by the time Malachi penned his book (early- to mid-400s BC), Obadiah's prophecy in verses 2–10 and 15–16 had been fulfilled. The Babylonians had already destroyed Edom. So it's no surprise when the Lord talks to Malachi about how He's, "laid waste [Esau's] mountains and his heritage for the jackals of the wilderness." When the Edomites claimed they would rebuild, God came back with, "I will throw down," and when

> And [Edom] shall be as though they had not been.
> And there shall not be any remaining of the house of Esau; for the Lord hath spoken it.
> (Obadiah 16b, 18b)

God issues a throwdown, is there even a contest (Mal. 1:2–5)? Yeah, I don't think so.

In your Bible, if you flip a page past the last one in the short book of Malachi, you'll find a yawning hole of silence. Actually, you'll probably see a title page for the New Testament, but right there, deep in the Bible's crease, lie 400 years of nothing from God. He says nothing about anything to anyone, including Edom. Why that is, is another study for another day. Suffice it to say, the next we hear of the delinquent kingdom of Edom is in Mark, and it isn't even called Edom anymore (Mark 3:7–8).

In the Hellenistic Period (the 300-ish years of Greek rule, starting in 321 BC), the region of Edom became known by the Greek version of its name, Idumea.[2] That region was Southern Judah, which had become so heavily populated with the now-called Idumeans, it took on the same name. Hold onto that fact for a few paragraphs, okay?

As for the area around Petra, which was traditionally Edomite lands, an Arabic tribe called the Nabataens (descendants of Ishmael) moved in and established themselves so thoroughly that all Edomite names around those parts gave way to Arabic.

Do you see it happening? God swiping His giant eraser over the chalkboard of history? What used to be the crisp white lines of the name Edom is fast becoming a smear of white with only a faint impression left behind. Forget nails on a chalkboard, the smeary powdery mess left behind by the eraser always makes me grit my teeth. But God is more thorough than my professor's eraser.

Moving on into Roman times, we have Israel reformed into five administrative districts. These were Roman tributaries overseen by a Roman procurator.[3] The Jews were allowed to govern themselves to a certain extent, which is how the Hasmonean leader John Hyrcanus, had the power to drive the Idumeans out of Southern Judah during his rule (143–102 BC).

According to renowned historian Josephus, after Hyrcanus thoroughly conquered the Edomites, he made the men receive circumcision. Here it is, straight from the horse's mouth:

> Hyrcanus took also Dora and Marissa, cities of Idumea, and subdued all the Idumeans; and permitted them to stay in that country, if they would circumcise their genitals, and make use of the laws of the Jews; and they were so desirous of living in the country of their forefathers, that they submitted to the use of circumcision, and of the rest of the Jewish ways of living; at which time therefore this befell them, that they were hereafter no other than Jews.[4]

Is anyone else shuddering with shock? The Edomites' choice to submit to circumcision effectively absorbed Esau's descendants into the kingdom of Judah, and any lines that remained between the two people groups were almost instantly blurred away. Didn't I say you wouldn't see it coming?

> And [Edom] shall be as though they had not been. And
> there shall not be any remaining of the house of Esau;
> for the Lord hath spoken it. (Obadiah 16b, 18b)

The repeated blocks of verse aren't an editorial blunder but an author trying to make a point. The Lord spoke, and history watched His promises unfold.

One more, then we'll move on.

The last official reference we have to Idumeans comes in the form of Antipater, the father of the Herodian rulers. Their dynasty included names you'll recognize from the Gospels and Paul's letters, such as Antipater's son, Herod the Great (ruled 37 BC to 4 AD), and others like Herod Antipas and Herod Agrippa. Where's the connection to Edom? The Roman historian Josephus names Antipas as one of those forced to convert to Judaism under Hyrcanus.[5]

When I learned this, I was confused for a second, thinking the Edomites had actually won the day, the throne, the ultimate victory. But nope. As Josephus said, "They were hereafter no other than Jews." Foreigners who converted to Judaism as the Idumeans did under Hyrcanus were called "proselytes of justice."[6]

According to Jewish tradition, this meant they'd gone through a number of rituals including circumcision, baptism, presentation of an offering, and vowing to observe the whole Mosaic law. Those acts gave them all the privileges of God's people and, technically, made them indistinguishable from those who'd been born Jews.[7] The Herodians' blood was traceable to Esau, but in the eyes of the law, they were full-fledged Jews.[8] (Although, I cannot imagine they were ever truly welcomed into the community.)

In the true spirit of righteous judgment, those three promises were completed: Edom was set afire and reduced to archaeological stubble, then Judah *devoured them*. "For the Lord hath spoken it" (Obad. 18b).

To this day, not a soul can trace their lineage back to Esau. And yet, because they had officially become Jews, they were "called by [His] name" (Amos 9:12). What a beautiful picture of hope and redemption and a perfect segue into how verses 17–18 are yet to be fulfilled.

C) Blessings and Promises (far fulfillment)

It's hard to argue that verses 17–18 haven't experienced a certain degree of fulfillment, but when we expand the Numbers reference to Edom (mentioned in the last chapter) to include the few verses leading up to it, we're forced to stall here and reconsider.

> I shall see him, but not now: I shall behold him, but not nigh: there shall come a Star out of Jacob, and a Sceptre shall rise out of Israel, and shall smite the corners of Moab, and destroy all the children of Sheth. And Edom shall be a possession, Seir also shall be a possession for his enemies; and Israel shall do valiantly. Out of Jacob shall come he that shall

184

have dominion, and shall destroy him that remaineth of the city. (Num. 24:17–19)

So what's all this about? First, pull out that pencil and mark any reference to Esau's descendants. You should find two.

Yep. Edom and Seir.

Okay, now underline the royal symbols mentioned. Hint: they're capitalized.

There they are: Star and Scepter. But who do they mean? King David? And what city does Balaam mean?

In all honesty, it's the strangest prophecy. Coming out of left field, it leaves a girl scratching her head. There's a strong argument here for King David since he defeated the Moabites and brought the Edomites under subjugation (2 Sam. 8). But those royal symbols could mean another King, and we all know His name.

Isaiah called the Messiah "a great light," and Jesus fulfilled that prophecy (Isa. 9:2; Matt. 4:14–16; John 8:12; Luke 1:79; John 1:8–9). Then there's one of my favorite names for Him: "I am the root and the offspring of David, and the *bright and morning star*" (Rev. 22:16b; 2 Peter 1:19). For references to Jesus as a Scepter, read Genesis 49:10 and Psalm 1:8.

Why am I getting down in the weeds on all this, and on a prophecy from wicked Balaam, no less? Because his oracle likely points to a future event, a *far* fulfillment, one our world has yet to see, and if Obadiah's prophecy was fully completed, Edom wouldn't be named as a part of that future (Num. 24:18).

This means that those blessings and the promises we've been discussing have more to them than what is immediately apparent. So typical of God's Word. And so very cool.

Moving into Obadiah 19–21 will confirm that. For all my dread of these verses, they have quickly become my favorites. In the next chapter, you'll see why.

Pop Quiz:

Put these kingdom-obliterating events in proper order:

- Hyrcanus forces circumcision, converting all Edomites into Jews
- Edomites become Idumeans
- Babylon invades and destroys Edom
- Idumeans driven out of Southern Judah
- Nabataens move in and all Edomite names become Arabic

19

Big, Big Picture

And the kingdom shall be the Lord's.
Obadiah 21b

This is it, girls, the last little chunk of Obadiah. Are you as sad as I am? It's been so much fun unwrapping this beautiful little book, but the best is yet to come.

These last few verses are the Ultimate Word of Hope. Yeah, I just made that term up. But really, how else can a person describe a declaration of Messiah's glorious, kingly return to Earth?

You're going too fast, April. Hit the back-up flashers.

Okay, remember the "possess the possessions" phrase from a couple verses up? We said that could mean when the Jews returned from Babylon and retook the land, rebuilt the walls and the Temple, all that. Sure, *those* verses could definitely mean that. The events fit.

But as Believers in a big, big God, we'd be silly to not pan out and scan for the big, big picture. In these last three verses, that's exactly what we have. The picture is so big that when I first began this study my brain couldn't hold all the pieces together, much less arrange them into the semblance of anything that made sense. Thank the Lord for the smarty brains with the PhDs who dedicate their lives to studying the Word.

> And they of the south shall possess the mount of Esau; and they of the plain the Philistines: and they shall possess the fields of Ephraim, and the fields of Samaria: and Benjamin shall possess Gilead. And the captivity of this host of the children of Israel shall possess that of the Canaanites, even unto Zarephath; and the captivity of Jerusalem, which is in Sepharad, shall possess the cities of the south.
> (Obadiah 19–20)

Turns out, I wasn't thinking big enough. I'd limited my thinking to an earthly timeline and political boundaries when I should have been thinking earth-wide rule by a universal Messiah.[1]

I'll spare you the mind-numbing details of boundaries and markers (current and historical), but Obadiah 19–20 reflect the promises given to Abraham, Moses, and Joshua (Gen. 15:18–21; Num. 34:1–12; Josh. 1:4). The lands listed in those verses were never fully possessed.

King David battled endlessly to expand the kingdom's borders and fulfill the promise. He and his son Solomon brought the kingdom to its greatest height of power and wealth (1 Chron.

29:25), but even they failed to eradicate the pagan nations. David did manage to subdue the Philistines (one of the kingdoms named in Obadiah 19), even taking control of Metheg Ammah, but he never fully absorbed their land into Israel (2 Sam. 8:1).

After their return from Babylon, they remained under the thumbs of larger empires (Babylon, Rome, etc.) and were never in a position to try again for expansion to their God-given boundaries. For example, "The South," a promised territory, in Obadiah 19–20 refers to the Negev.

In the previous chapter, we learned that in the era after the Jews' release from Babylonian captivity, the Nabataens dominated the Negev until they lost it to Romans in 106 AD. Today, Israel controls 97 percent of the Negev, but that's a recent development, and their borders don't extend to the Nile or the Euphrates, as promised.

The modern State of Israel was formed in 1948, a direct fulfillment of prophecy in Isaiah 66:8, but if they were ever to get inspired to conquer their ancient Promised Land, they would have to invade Egypt, Lebanon, Jordan, Sudan, Syria, Iraq, and part of Turkey.[2] Then there's Gaza and the West Bank, which they only partially control.

All these facts push the relevance of these final verses in Obadiah far out from Obadiah's times, from Babylonian times, and even past our own time. How far past is always the question, isn't it? We'll leave that in God's capable hands. All we should concern ourselves with is the fact that "they shall possess."

Since God speaks the phrase no less than *seven times* over those final verses, it's safe to say, He's trying to drive home a very important point.

Israel shall possess!

What a glorious reassurance this repeated declaration would have been to the enslaved Jews. If it feels like a ticker-tape parade to me (as I sit in my comfy chair in my safe home in my perfect freedom), I can only imagine how they must have taken it. If they didn't blare trumpets and take to the streets to dance before the Lord with all their might (2 Sam. 6:14–15), it was only because their Babylonian captors were party-poopers and didn't allow it.

But it gets better.

The captives that this book was written for would have been understandably shortsighted as they looked forward to their physical return to Judah to rebuild Jerusalem and watch Edom fall. No one can fault them that. But from where we're standing in the 21st century, we can see that *there's so much more.*

The book of Obadiah takes a journey through literal history. Literal invasions. Literal temples going up in literal smoke. Literal people betraying, capturing, and killing other literal people. It makes sense that these last verses should be read the same way. There will come a day when Israel will literally control all the named lands.

Literal saviors (generals) under a literal General, after having conquered literal kingdoms, will march to a literal Mount Zion to sit in literal judgment. Isaiah 63:1–4 states that Messiah will be Edom's final judge. Obadiah reiterates that in verse 21, then goes on to make a conclusion statement that sends chills up my arms every time I read it.

AND THE KINGDOM SHALL BE THE LORD'S.

Call me dramatic. That's fine. If there's anything to get big-font, all-caps about, it's the return of our Savior Jesus Christ. Can I get a hanky-raising hallelujah?

> And saviours shall come up on mount Zion to judge the mount of Esau; and the kingdom shall be the Lord's. (Obadiah 21)

Throughout Scripture, God continues to address this. Here's Jeremiah on the subject: "But the Lord is the true God; He is the living God and the everlasting King. At His wrath the earth will tremble, And the nations will not be able to endure His indignation" (Jer. 10:10). Don't know about you, but I'm pretty stoked about worshipping a God powerful enough to rattle a giant spinning ball of dirt. If nothing else, it's good incentive to make sure we're on the correct side of His wrath and indignation.

When Zechariah speaks of the Day of the Lord, he says, "And in that day it shall be that living waters shall flow from Jerusalem...and the Lord shall be King over all the earth" (Zech. 14:8–9). Not "over all Jerusalem" or "over Israel" or even "the Middle East." But OVER ALL THE

EARTH. Hang on, my dear friend. The Day of the Lord is coming.

All of Solomon's prophetic Psalm 72 is worth a read and a triumphant shout, but verse 8 sums it up by stating, "He [Messiah] shall have dominion also from sea to sea, and from the River to the ends of the earth." No political boundaries here.

How about we go out with a bang?

"And He has on His robe and on His thigh a name written: KING OF KINGS AND LORD OF LORDS" (Rev. 19:16). It doesn't get more beautiful than that, but Obadiah's "And the kingdom shall be the Lord's" comes pretty close.

Seatwork:

Unfamiliar with the 1948 Arab-Israeli War and the particulars of how the State of Israel was formed? I encourage you to read up on it. If you're like me and enjoying learning through historical fiction, check out Brock and Bodie Thoene's Zion Chronicles. Excellent reads.

Go deeper with *But in Mount Zion*:
- Read "But in Mount Zion."
- Quote: Despite Mount Zion's 4,000 years of historical, political, and spiritual significance, those who know Christ as Savior may legitimately identify with it. But calling Jerusalem our King's future throne is only the beginning. What about between now and then? Today, I ask, "Who are you, daughter of Zion?"

What to Read Next
in the *A Fire and a Flame* series

- ✓ *A Hope Fulfilled*, a novella of biblical Edom and Obadiah's prophecy
- ✓ *Knowing Obadiah*, a Christian Women's Bible Commentary
- ✓ *But in Mount Zion*, a companion study (personal or small group) for *Knowing Obadiah*

Can be read in any order.
Learn More / Purchase:
www.aprilgardner.com/fireandflame.

Visit the author's website for these gifts:

1. a printable download of "Edom's Interactions with Israel," a compilation of Scripture from Genesis to Mark, listing Israel's dealings with Edom
2. a link to the live recording of the unexpected end of the 38-year squabble between April and her sister over the rubber stamp, inspired by this book's creation. Whose was it *really*? In this video, we find out.

www.aprilgardner.com/fireandflame-freebies

About the Author

APRIL W GARDNER is an editor and award-winning author of Christian fiction. She lives in South Texas with her husband and two German shepherds. April dreams of owning a horse, learning a third language, and visiting all the national parks.

Series Acknowlegments

As ever, God gets first credit. Thank you, Lord, for the inspiration and for providing every word of this series.

Mom, literally couldn't have done it without you. Your experience, wisdom, and insightful content helped make this series what it is. I'm proud to put your name next to mine on the cover of *But in Mount Zion.*

Others who contributed with invaluable feedback and who deserve oodles of thanks: my faithful writing partners Tanya Eavenson and Rebekah Gyger, my brilliant editor Lesley McDaniel, and advanced readers Dr. Susan Rosenburg, Charlotte, Susan, Jennifer W., and Jennifer C. Thank you each for your time, your input, and your dedication to excellence.

Pop Quiz Answers

Chapter 3

1. False. No one knows for sure when Obadiah was written, but most scholars place the writing between 588 and 550 BC.
2. 587 BC. April has chosen 587 BC because scriptural and historical evidence outside of Obadiah lean heavily that way.
3. Bingo! You got it. There you go, sister. They think it was mine, too. ;-)

Chapter 4

For me, the most memorable "thus saith the Lord" passages are Moses's interactions with Pharoah found in Exodus 4–11. "Thus saith the Lord, Let my people go, that they may serve me" (Exod. 8:1b).

Chapter 5

Edom was named for its red sandstone and for its redheaded forefather, Esau (Gen. 25:25).

Chapter 11

The Roman soldiers casting lots for Jesus's garment is indisputably the most notable instance of that practice in the Bible (Matt. 27:35). Another one that comes to mind right off is Jonah when the sailors were trying to decide which passenger had angered the gods and brought on the terrible storm (Jon. 1:7).

Chapter 13

Obadiah's intended audience was the Judeans because of the violent Edomites who dwell next to the nesting eagles on the heights.

Chapter 14

David: "Yea, mine own familiar friend, in whom I trusted, which did eat of my bread, hath lifted up his heel against me" (Ps. 41:9).

Jesus: "Now when the even was come, he sat down with the twelve And as they did eat, he said, Verily I say unto you, that one of you shall betray me" (Matt. 26:20–21).

Chapter 16

One of Job's friends was a Temanite. "Now when Job's three friends heard of all this evil that was come upon him, they came every one from his own place; Eliphaz the Temanite, and Bildad the Shuhite, and Zophar the Naamathite: for they had made an appointment together to come to mourn with him and to comfort him" (Job 2:11).

Chapter 18

Put these kingdom-obliterating events in proper order.

1. Babylon invades and destroys
2. Edomites become Idumeans
3. Nabataens move in and all Edomite names become Arabic
4. Idumeans driven out of Southern Judah
5. Hyrcanus forces circumcision, converting all Edomites into Jews

Edom Through the Ages

For those of you who prefer to approach a thing with a broad view, here's Edom at a glance (key events underlined).[1]

To orient you, the kingdom's existence spanned from around 1926 BC to 550 BC. The early dates are approximate, but they become more reliable the further into the timeline we go. For example, there's little dispute about the date of Babylon's invasion of Jerusalem (587 BC). From there, you can trust the dates are accurate, especially once we enter Roman times (27 BC).

- Esau's birth (2006–1836 BC)
- Esau sells his birthright to Jacob
- Esau marries four women and has five sons in Canaan
- Esau loses his blessing to Jacob, threatens to kill Jacob
- Esau conquers the Horites at Seir (Deut. 2:12)
- Birth of Edom, the nation
- Esau and Jacob reconcile (twenty-one years later)
- Esau moves his entire holdings to Seir
- Egypt/Exodus
- Edom refuses to allow the Children of Israel to pass through their land
- Edom in continual conflict with Israel and Judah (900–795 BC)
- Edom appoints a formal king

- Edom, Israel, Syria, and Philistia attack Jerusalem
- Edom in alliance with kings of Moab, Ammon, Tyre, Sidon, and Jerusalem to defend against Babylon in 595 BC (Jer. 27:3)
- Babylonian invasion of Israel 587 BC
- Edom aids Babylon in the destruction of Jerusalem and burning of Solomon's Temple (Jer. 52:12–13)
- Edom condemned: Obadiah, Jeremiah, Ezekiel
- Edom spreads into the Negev after Babylon carries off Judah into captivity (587 BC)
- Edom is driven from their ancient lands by Arabs and relocates entirely to Negev (550 BC)
- Edom called Idumea and Temple rebuilt (520 BC)
- Edom predicted to become an extinct nation (Mal. 1:1–5)
- Edomites forced into circumcision by Maccabean leader and High Priest John Hycranus (135–104 BC)
- Idumea controlled by Jews during their brief period of independence (110–63 BC)
- Idumeans follow Jesus (Mark 3:7–8) (AD 28)
- Idumeans participate with rebels during the First Jewish War (AD 68)
- Idumean homeland (Negev) destroyed by Emperor Vespasian (AD 68)
- Temple Destroyed (AD 70)
- Near extinction of Edomites (destroyed along with 1.1 million Jews in Jerusalem, AD 70)

Sources

CHAPTER 1: Bird's Eye Verses
1. David Guzik, "Malachi 1," *The Enduring Word Commentary*. Local View Digital Marketing, *Enduring Word*, 2023, enduringword.com/bible-commentary/malachi-1/.
2. "Obadiah," *The Bible Project*, BibleProject, 7 May 2016, https://bibleproject.com/explore/video/obadiah/.

CHAPTER 2: Meet and Greet
1. John Calvin, *Twelve Minor Prophets*. Calvin's Commentaries 22-Volume Set, vol. 2, pg. vi, Baker Books, 2003.

CHAPTER 3: Timeline Talk
1. April Gardner, "A Brief History of Edom and Its Interactions with Israel." Big Spring Press, 2023.

CHAPTER 4: Ambassador's Announcement
1. James Strong, *The Exhaustive Concordance of the Bible*. A Concise Dictionary of the Words in the Hebrew Bible, pg. 118, Hendrickson Publishers, 2009.
2. April Gardner, "Rise Up Against Her for Battle." Big Spring Press, 2023.

CHAPTER 5: Introducing Edom
1. "Kingdoms of the Levant, 9th century BC." See "List of Citations," *Knowing Obadiah*, p. 189.
2. Alan R. Millard, "Obadiah." *Zondervan Illustrated Bible Backgrounds Commentary*, vol. 5, p. 91. Walton, John H., editor. Zondervan, 2009.
3. Israel Finkelstein, "Khirbet En-Nahas, Edom and Biblical History." Tel Aviv (1974), vol. 32, no. 1, 2005, pp. 119–25, doi.org/10.1179/tav.2005.2005.1.119.

4. Benjamin W. Porter, "Authority, Polity, and Tenuous Elites in Iron Age Edom (Jordon)." *Oxford Journal of Archaeology*, vol. 23, no. 4, 2004, pp. 373–95, doi.org/10.1111/j.1468-0092.2004.00216.

5. Alan R. Millard, "Obadiah." *Zondervan Illustrated Bible Backgrounds Commentary*, vol. 5. Walton, John H., editor. Zondervan, 2009.

6. Nelson Glueck, "The Second Campaign at Tell El-Kheleifeh (Ezion-Geber: Elath)." *Bulletin of the American Schools of Oriental Research, no. 75, 1939, pp. 8–22. JSTOR, doi.org/10.2307/3218784.*

7. Edward Lipinski, "Edom at the Crossroads of 'Incense Routes' in the 8th–7th Centuries B.C." *Rocznik Orientalistyczny/Yearbook of Oriental Studies*, No. 2, 2013.

8. "Neo-Babylonia at Its Height." IchthyovenatorSémhur (base map), CC BY-SA 4.0 <https://creativecommons.org/licenses/by-sa/4.0>, via Wikimedia Commons.

CHAPTER 6: The Troublesome Twins

1. "Despise." *Merriam-Webster*, Merriam-Webster Incorporated, 2022, www.merriam-webster.com/dictionary/despise.

2. Benjamin W. Porter, "Authority, Polity, and Tenuous Elites in Iron Age Edom (Jordon)." *Oxford Journal of Archaeology*, vol. 23, no. 4, 2004, pp. 381, doi.org/10.1111/j.1468-0092.2004.00216.

3. "Edomite_Goddess." https://commons.wikimedia.org/wiki/File:-0650_Edomite_Goddess_from_Horvat_Qitmit._Israel_Museum,_Jerusalem_anagoria.jpg.

4. Vergilius Ture Anselm Ferm, *Forgotten Religions, Including Some Living Primitive Religions*. Books for Libraries Press, 1970. pp 83−88.

CHAPTER 9: Blessing-Curse-Prophecy

1. "Genesis 27:39," *Bible Hub*, Bible Hub: Search, Read, Study the Bible in Many Languages, 2022, https://biblehub.com/genesis/27-39.htm.

2. "Genesis 27:40," *Bible Hub*, Bible Hub: Search, Read, Study the Bible in Many Languages, 2022, https://biblehub.com/genesis/27-40.htm#lexicon.

3. "Genesis 27," *Bible Hub*, Bible Hub: Search, Read, Study the Bible in Many Languages, 2022, https://biblehub.com/commentaries/kad/genesis/27.htm.

4. Flavius Josephus, *Josephus, the Complete Works*, "Antiquities of the Jews — Book XIII," https://penelope.uchicago.edu/josephus/ant-13.html.

CHAPTER 10: Tumbling Temple

1. Richard N Fry, "Nebuchadrezzar II." *Britannica*, www.britannica.com/place/Mesopotamia-historical-region-Asia/Nebuchadrezzar-II.

2. Hillel Geva, "Jerusalem's Population in Antiquity: A Minimalist View." Tel Aviv (1974), vol. 41, no. 2, 2014, p. 11, doi.org/10.1179/0334435514Z.00000000041.

3. "Who was Nebuzaradan in the Bible?" *GotQuestions*, Got Questions Ministries, 2022, www.gotquestions.org/Nebuzaradan.html.

CHAPTER 13: Mic Drop

1. E.W. Bullinger, *Figures of speech used in the Bible, explained and illustrated by E. W. Bullinger*. Eyre & Spottiswoode; E. & J.B. Young & co., p. 518, 1898.

2. Benjamin W. Porter, "Authority, Polity, and Tenuous Elites in Iron Age Edom (Jordon)." *Oxford Journal of Archaeology*, vol. 23, no. 4, 2004, pp. 377–78, doi.org/10.1111/j.1468-0092.2004.00216.

3. Nelson Glueck, "THE BOUNDARIES OF EDOM." Hebrew Union College Annual, vol. 11, 1936, pp. 148. JSTOR, www.jstor.org/stable/23503134.

CHAPTER 16: Nabonidus Was Here

1. Bradley L Crowell, "Nabonidus, as-Silaʿ, and the Beginning of the End of Edom." *Bulletin of the American Schools of Oriental Research*, vol. 348, no. 348, 2007, pp. 75–88, doi.org/10.1086/BASOR25067039.

2. "Basalt Stela of Nabonidus." British Museum, CC BY 3.0 <https://creativecommons.org/licenses/by/3.0>, via Wikimedia Commons.

3. Morgan Gardner, "Babylonian Cuneiform, as Sila Inscription." Adapted from Gentili and Saporetti (2001), 2022.

4. "Bradley L Crowell, "Nabonidus, as-Silaʿ, and the Beginning of the End of Edom." *Bulletin of the American Schools of Oriental Research*, vol. 348, no. 348, 2007, pp. 75–88, doi.org/10.1086/BASOR25067039.

5. April Gardner, *A Hope Fulfilled.* Big Spring Press, p. 19, 2023.

CHAPTER 18: Three Promises

1. Morgan Gardner, "Dumb Hooman." Big Spring Press, 2023.

2. "Idumea," *Bible Hub*, Bible Hub: Search, Read, Study the Bible in Many Languages, 2022, https://biblehub.com/topical/i/idumea.htm.

3. Lawrence H. Schiffman, "The Land of Israel Under Roman Rule." *My Jewish Learning*, My Jewish Learning, 2022. www.myjewishlearning.com/article/palestine-under-roman-rule/. 3. Flavius Josephus, *Josephus, the Complete Works*, "Chapter 9. How, After the Death of Antiochus…," *Christian Classics Ethereal Library*, Harry Plantinga, 2022, https://www.ccel.org/ccel/josephus/complete.ii.xiv.ix.html

4. Flavius Josephus, *Josephus, the Complete Works*, "Chapter 9. How, After the Death of Antiochus…,"

Christian Classics Ethereal Library, Harry Plantinga, 2022, www.ccel.org/ccel/josephus/complete.ii.xiv.ix.html.

5. Flavius Josephus, *Josephus, the Complete Works*, "Chapter 9. How, After the Death of Antiochus…," *Christian Classics Ethereal Library*, Harry Plantinga, 2022, ccel.org/ccel/josephus/complete/complete.ii.xv.i.html#fnf_ ii.xv.i-p4.1.

6. "Proselyte." *StudyLight*, StudyLight.org, 2022, www.studylight.org/dictionaries/eng/wtd/p/proselyte.html.

7. "Proselyte." *Encyclopedic Dictionary of Bible and Theology*, Biblia.Work, 2022, www.biblia.work/dictionaries/proselyte/.

8. Gassner, Evie. "How Jewish Was Herod?" *The Torah*, Project TABS, 2022, www.thetorah.com/article/how-jewish-was-herod.

CHAPTER 19: Big, Big Picture

1. Clarence Johnson. "Every Square Inch!" *Israel My Glory*, The Friends of Israel Gospel Ministry, April 2015, https://israelmyglory.org/article/every-square-inch/.

2. "Has Israel's territory ever encompassed the promise in Joshua 1:4?" *GotQuestions*, Got Questions Ministries, 2022, www.gotquestions.org/Israel-territory.html.

EDOM THROUGH THE AGES

1. "The Edomites." The Interactive Bible, *Bible.ca*, March 2020, www.bible.ca/archeology/bible-archeology-edomite-territory-mt-seir.htm#I.

List of Citations

Bullinger, E. W. *Figures of speech used in the Bible, explained and illustrated by E. W. Bullinger*. Eyre & Spottiswoode; E. & J.B. Young & co., p. 518, 1898.

Calvin, John. *Twelve Minor Prophets*. Calvin's Commentaries 22-Volume Set, vol. 2. Baker Books, 2003.

Crowell, Bradley L. "Nabonidus, as-Silaʿ, and the Beginning of the End of Edom." *Bulletin of the American Schools of Oriental Research*, vol. 348, no. 348, 2007, pp. 75–88, doi.org/10.1086/BASOR25067039.

"Despise." *Merriam-Webster*, Merriam-Webster Incorporated, 2022, https://www.merriam-webster.com/dictionary/despise.

Ferm, Vergilius Ture Anselm. *Forgotten Religions, Including Some Living Primitive Religions*. Books for Libraries Press, 1970. pp 83−88.

Finkelstein, Israel. "Khirbet En-Nahas, Edom and Biblical History." Tel Aviv (1974), vol. 32, no. 1, 2005, pp. 119–25, https://doi.org/10.1179/tav.2005.2005.1.119.

Fry, Richard N. "Nebuchadrezzar II." *Britannica*, https://www.britannica.com/place/Mesopotamia-historical-region-Asia/Nebuchadrezzar-II.

Gassner, Evie. "How Jewish Was Herod?" *The Torah*, Project TABS, 2022, https://www.thetorah.com/article/how-jewish-was-herod.

"Genesis 27," *Bible Hub*, Bible Hub: Search, Read, Study the Bible in Many Languages, 2022, https://biblehub.com/commentaries/kad/genesis/27.htm.

Ibid. "Genesis 27:40," biblehub.com/genesis/27-40.htm#lexicon.

Ibid. "Genesis 27:38," biblehub.com/commentaries/genesis/27-38.htm.

Ibid. "Idumea," biblehub.com/topical/i/idumea.htm.

Armerding, Thomas E. "Obadiah." *The Expositor's Bible Commentary*, Vol. 7, Gaebelein, Frank E., editor. Zondervan, 1985.

Gardner, April. *A Hope Fulfilled*. Big Spring Press, p. 19, 2023.

Geva, Hillel. "Jerusalem's Population in Antiquity: A Minimalist View." Tel Aviv (1974), vol. 41, no. 2, 2014, p. 11, doi.org/10.1179/0334435514Z.00000000041.

Glueck, Nelson. "THE BOUNDARIES OF EDOM." Hebrew Union College Annual, vol. 11, 1936, pp. 148. JSTOR, www.jstor.org/stable/23503134.

Glueck, Nelson. "The Second Campaign at Tell El-Kheleifeh (Ezion-Geber: Elath)." *Bulletin of the American Schools of Oriental Research*, no. 75, 1939, pp. 8–22. JSTOR, doi.org/10.2307/3218784.

Guzik, Davi. "Jeremiah: Bonds and Yokes." *Enduring Word*, The Enduring Word Bible Commentary, 2021, https://enduringword.com/bible-commentary/jeremiah-27/.

"Has Israel's territory ever encompassed the promise in Joshua 1:4?" *GotQuestions*, Got Questions Ministries, 2022, www.gotquestions.org/Israel-territory.html.

Johnson, Clarence. "Every Square Inch!" *Israel My Glory*, The Friends of Israel Gospel Ministry, April 2015, https://israelmyglory.org/article/every-square-inch/.

Josephus, Flavius. *Josephus, the Complete Works*, "Antiquities of the Jews — Book XIII," https://penelope.uchicago.edu/josephus/ant-13.html.

Josephus, Flavius. *Josephus, the Complete Works*, "Chapter 9. How, After the Death of Antiochus…," *Christian Classics Ethereal Library*, Harry Plantinga, 2022, www.ccel.org/ccel/josephus/complete.ii.xiv.ix.html.

Ibid. ccel.org/ccel/josephus/complete/complete.ii.xv.i.html #fnf_ii.xv.i-p4.1.

Lipinski, Edward, "Edom at the Crossroads of 'Incense Routes,'" *Rocznik Orientalistyczny/Yearbook of Oriental Studies*, No. 2, 2013.

Millard, Alan R. "Obadiah." *Zondervan Illustrated Bible Backgrounds Commentary*, vol. 5. Walton, John H., editor. Zondervan, 2009.

Porter, Benjamin W. "Authority, Polity, and Tenuous Elites in Iron Age Edom (Jordon)." *Oxford Journal of Archaeology*, vol. 23, no. 4, 2004, pp. 373–95, doi.org/10.1111/j.1468-0092.2004.00216.x.

"Proselyte." *Encyclopedic Dictionary of Bible and Theology*, Biblia.Work, 2022, www.biblia.work/dictionaries/proselyte/.

"Proselyte." *StudyLight*, StudyLight.org, 2022, www.studylight.org/dictionaries/eng/wtd/p/proselyte.html.

Schiffman, Lawrence H. "The Land of Israel Under Roman Rule." *My Jewish Learning*, My Jewish Learning, 2022, myjewishlearning.com/article/palestine-under-roman-rule/.

"Summary of the Book of Obadiah," *GotQuestions*, Got Questions Ministries, 2022, www.gotquestions.org/Book-of-Obadiah.html.

"The Edomites." The Interactive Bible, *Bible.ca*, March 2020, www.bible.ca/archeology/bible-archeology-edomite-territory-mt-seir.htm#I.

"Who was Nebuzaradan in the Bible?" *GotQuestions*, Got Questions Ministries, 2022, www.gotquestions.org/Nebuzaradan.html.

Illustration Attributions

"A Brief History of Edom and Its Interactions with Israel." Gardner, April. Big Spring Press, 2023.

"Babylonian Cuneiform, as Sila Inscription." Gardner, Morgan. Adapted from Gentili and Saporetti (2001), 2022.

"Basalt Stela of Nabonidus." British Museum, CC BY 3.0 creativecommons.org/licenses/by/3.0>, via Wikimedia Commons.

"Dumb Hooman." Gardner, M. Big Spring Press, 2023.

"Edomite_Goddess." https://commons.wikimedia.org/wiki/File:-0650_Edomite_Goddess_from_Horvat_Qitmit._Israel_Museum,_Jerusalem_anagoria.jpg.

"Kingdoms of the Levant, 9th century BC." Kingdoms_around_Israel_830_map.svg: *Kingdoms_of_Israel_and_Judah_map_830.svg: *Oldtidens_Israel_&_Judea.svg: FinnWikiNoderivative work: Richardprins (talk)derivative work: Richardprins (talk)Kingdoms_of_Israel_and_Judah_map_830.svg: *Oldtidens_Israel_&_Judea.svg: FinnWikiNoderivative work: Richardprins (talk)derivative work: Dlv999, CC BY-SA 3.0 <https://creativecommons.org/licenses/by-sa/3.0>, via Wikimedia Commons.

"Neo-Babylonia at Its Height." IchthyovenatorSémhur (base map), CC BY-SA 4.0 <https://creativecommons.org/licenses/by-sa/4.0>, via Wikimedia Commons.

"Rise Up Against Her for Battle." Gardner, April. Big Spring Press, 2023.